A Treasury of One-Line Gems

White is a symbol of happiness. Could that be the reason a groom always wears black?

A thirty-fifth wedding anniversary is difficult to celebrate. It's too soon to brag and too late to complain.

A woman is generally as old as she looks, and then some.

A girl will go to any length to change her width.

When a youngster hears a bad word, it goes in one ear—and out his mouth.

2,000 ONE-LINERS was originally published by Trident Press.

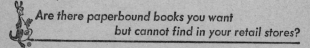

2000 ONE LINERS

Compiled by
Larry Oliver

Illustrated by John Huehnergarth

PUBLISHED BY POCKET BOOKS NEW YORK

2,000 ONE-LINERS

Trident Press edition published October, 1969

Pocket Book edition published December, 1970

This *Pocket Book* edition includes every word
contained in the original, higher-priced edition. It is printed
from brand-new plates made from completely reset, clear, easy-to-read
type. *Pocket Book* editions are published by Pocket Books, a division
of Simon & Schuster, Inc., 630 Fifth Avenue, New York, N.Y. 10020.
Trademarks registered in the United States and other countries.

L

CONTENTS

ADOLESCENCE

ADOLESCENT: A youngster old enough to dress himself if he could just remember where he dropped his clothes.

*

The way we figger, adolescence is that period when many kids feel their parents should be told the facts of life.

*

Adolescence is when boys discover girls, and girls discover they've been discovered.

*

ADOLESCENCE: The time in a boy's life when he notices that a girl notices he is noticing her.

*

When the youngsters begin to question the answers, adolescence has set in.

*

The good Lord gives pimples to adolescents to teach them humility—without pimples they'd be insufferable.

*

When a girl begins to powder and a boy begins to puff, that's adolescence.

*

Usually an adolescent is a minor with a major problem.

*

Adolescence is when most fellows with a houseful of kids have a checkbook and a pen that writes under duress.

*

Despite the fantasies of adolescents, no kind of life is "wonderful" after you get used to it.

*

ADOLESCENCE: When a boy is less interested in Mary's little lamb than in her little limb.

*

Our private opinion is that when talking to wild teen-agers does no good, it's time to start threshing things out.

*

Let's face it. Adolescence is the awkward age in the life of a youngster. They're too old for an allowance and too young for a credit card.

*

ADOLESCENCE: That period in a boy's life when he refuses to believe that someday he'll be as dumb as his father.

*

Adolescence in the life of parents is when dad goes out to the garage and finds several little hairpins scattered here and there, gasoline deleted, and the tires. . . . Well, anyway, there's the faint perfume aroma, mudguards sprayed with tar, which all plainly shows that last night Junior had the car.

*

When your daughters begin putting on lipstick, and your sons begin wiping it off—on other girls—that, my friend, is adolescence. But whenever you feel like criticizing the kids, just remember who raised them. After all, you know, the only thing wrong with our youngsters in their adolescent age is that they're so much like the older generation was at their age.

*

Sometimes an adolescent is one who, when not treated like an adult, acts like an infant.

*

Some girls complain that they had no adolescence at all—they went right from baby fat to middle-age spread.

*

FACT: When "growing pains" begin to manifest themselves, the kids are getting big enough to wear your clothes.

*

Did you ever notice that the mere mention of a sinkful of dirty dishes will often inspire your adolescent youngsters to practice their piano lessons, or catch up on a little homework?

*

Adolescence is a period of rapid changes. Between the ages of twelve and seventeen, for example, a parent ages as much as twenty years.

*

When little girls stop making faces at the boys and start making eyes at them, then you know the age of adolescence has arrived.

*

An adolescent is anyone who is well informed about anything he doesn't have to study.

*

You can believe it or not, but adolescence is sometimes the period between hopscotch and real Scotch.

*

In adolescence, the boys seem to have a higher IQ than the girls, but the girls soon surpass them and at the age of about sixteen, it's neck and neck.

*

No one is as old as he hopes to be.

*

No matter how old we are, we still want to live to that ripe old age when the battle of the sexes is none of our affair.

*

We never realize it, of course, but among the things that aren't what they used to be—are we.

*

The Metallic Age is usually associated with mines, but some folks we know have also arrived at the "metallic age," with gold in their teeth, silver in their hair and lead in their pants.

*

Deep breathing adds to your longevity, especially if you can do it for eighty-five or ninety years.

*

Did you know that at the age of seventy-five there are 18 percent more women than men? But then at that age, who cares?

*

Youngsters don't seem to realize that it's just a matter of time until every young kid winds up as an old goat.

*

Our private opinion is that just because the engine is a little cold, it's no sign the anchor is dragging.

*

After a woman passes fifty, she is called upon to deny her weight as well as her age.

*

After sixty-five, never give your age a second thought.

*

By the time we learn to watch our step, we're not stepping out very much.

*

When we reach the age of about sixty, and have lived our life a little bit fast, all we can do is hum and buzz, and brag about what a helluva guy we was.

*

What Mother Nature giveth, Father Time taketh away.

*

Have you reached the age when you're losing a little on top? Well, cheer up! You're probably gaining in the middle.

*

The perfect example of arrested motion is a woman entering her thirties.

*

Women seldom suffer from any given age—except when it's given by another woman.

*

When we were twenty, we planned for what we would do at forty, but when we reach sixty or thereabouts, we plan for what we're going to do after breakfast.

*

Nature gave us the face we had at twenty, life modeled the face we had at thirty, but by the time we reach fifty and beyond, the face we have is the one we deserve.

*

The best years of your life are just about over when girls think your whistle is a whistle for Rover.

*

The way we figure, the difficult age is when we're too tired to work and too poor to quit.

*

How come folks never get too old to learn new ways to be stupid?

*

Threescore years and ten is the time allotted to man, and that should be enough. If he can't suffer all the misery he wants in that time, he must be numb.

*

A young fellow gets up full of pep and goes to bed rested. At middle age he gets up rested and goes to bed tired, but when he becomes old he gets up tired and goes to bed exhausted.

*

The man who goes like sixty when he's twenty seldom reaches forty.

*

When a pretty girl smiles at a man of twenty, he looks himself over to see what makes him so attractive. When a pretty young thing smiles at a man of forty, he looks around to see who the handsome fellow behind him is—but when a lady of any age smiles at a man of sixty, he looks down to see what's unzipped.

*

It's hell to be old when the night is young.

*

When you get too old to dream, check on your Social Security rights.

*

FACT: Maintain a youthful outlook and before you know it, people will be calling you a silly old man.

*

A man is getting well along in years when an old flame doesn't seem so hot.

*

Forty is the age when a woman stops patting herself on the back—and begins on the chin.

*

Many a girl becomes blue at the first sign of gray.

*

Nothing makes a woman older than having her friends discover when she was born.

*

Middle age is what most women often try to deny, but they finally have to meet it—with both chins flying high.

*

Time marches on, but most of the girls try to fall out of the parade.

*

FACT: It's never too late to mend, because the older we get the more repairs we need.

*

Nature is generous. When we reach the sitting-around stage of life, she provides us with more cushions.

*

The years between twenty-six and sixty pass as fast as the fuel in a teen-ager's gas tank.

*

You can figure your youth is gone beyond all doubt when you've got money to burn but the fire's gone out.

*

Don't you ever believe that an old boy is too old to worry about. Just remember that at the brewery they have to put the strongest lid on the oldest vat.

*

A lot of the fellows who are sixty actually look fifty. They act like forty, feel like thirty, and can see plenty of opportunities they overlooked at twenty. But then, after all, you know, a woman may be as old as she looks, but a man is old if he doesn't.

*

Most of us start out when we're young to find the pot at the end of the rainbow, but as the years advance all we've found is the pot.

*

Does the going seem a little easier lately? Better check. You just might be going downhill.

*

MIDDLE AGE: When the brain says, "Go! Go! Go!" while the rest of you is saying, "No! No! No!"

*

If you're over forty, do yourself a favor and stay out of discotheques. At this age it's no longer dancing. It's committing suicide, one bone at a time.

*

At sixteen we think only of fortunes; at sixty we think only of pensions.

*

With all the wonderful things medical science is doing to lengthen human life, it's a strange thing that they can't get a woman's life past forty.

*

A woman is generally as old as she looks, and then some.

*

In our private opinion, the most difficult age for any woman is the one she has to swear to.

*

You're still young if the morning after the night before still makes the night before worth the morning after.

*

When the girls start calling a man "Sir," about all he has to look forward to is Social Security.

*

This you'd better believe:
We're really getting old, as well as losing our zip and snap,
When a pretty girl gets on our nerves instead of on our lap.

*

In the younger years it's wine, women and song; but as the years take their toll, it's beer, the better half and television.

*

The saddest sight along the way
Is a playboy who is too old to play.

*

An authority on aging says that men are smartest at the age of fifty—which is precisely when there is nobody around the house who will listen to him.

*

Youth is that period when we're all looking for greener fields. Middle age is when we can hardly mow the one we've got.

*

AGE: That which makes wine worth more and women less.

*

Age is sneaking up when, after painting the town red, you need a long rest before applying the second coat.

*

A man has just about had it when his weight lifting consists of standing up.

*

MEN: Be glad you've passed forty. Women are still interested in you, but the Army isn't.

*

FACT: Normally, at the age of sixty, the biological urge slowly turns to an occasional nudge.

*

When a man is young and the winds are high,
He stands on the corner to watch the girls' skirts fly,
But when he's a bit feeble and kind of old,
High winds now just leave him cold.

He who paints the town red is often left holding the brush.

*

The trouble with painting the town red is that you wake up the next morning feeling as if you'd swallowed the turpentine.

*

There's many a man who paints the town red after his girl has given him the brush.

*

The fellow who starts his evening fast and loose generally comes home slow and tight.

*

Ain't it funny? When a fellow gets "lit" he always wants to go out.

*

Give some fellows Four Roses and they'll start talking flowery language. With others, a pony of brandy and they'll start to horse around.

*

The guy who orders a soft drink has no kick coming.

*

A kind word, please, for our heavy drinkers. They pay a big part of our taxes.

*

"Bottoms up" is not always changing the baby.

*

The pioneer women who fought grasshoppers on the plains now have great-granddaughters who drink them.

*

It's wine, women and gin
That make a fellow spin.

*

Men and money are a great deal alike. The tighter they get, the more they talk.

*

The way we figure, when anyone gets three sheets in the wind, he often becomes a wet blanket.

*

HANGOVER: When the dawn comes up like thunder.

*

Man is far from being a machine, yet he's seldom quiet when he's well oiled.

*

Some fellows drink only on the advice of their doctor. So when the bartender asks, "Have another?" the reply is, "You're the doctor!"

*

The trouble with a lot of folks who drink to forget is that they have a strong memory.

*

Liquor talks mighty loud when it gets loose in the jug.

*

There's nothing like a "toot" to start a fellow off on the wrong train of thought.

*

When a man gets high he always feels mighty.

*

It's awfully hard to follow the straight and narrow when you're on a bender.

*

A lot of fellows stagger home in the late hours, turn the key in the lock—and wonder what they're letting themselves in for.

*

When a man gets high as a kite he usually comes home with quite a tale.

*

Many a man goes into a bar for an eye-opener and comes out blind.

*

After a few drinks an old man can get quite a spring to his stagger.

*

Have you ever listened to what they promise you on those beer commercials? Man, it's like a bottled honeymoon.

*

"Swims" is what happens to your head when you drink too much.

*

The trouble with some folks who drink too much is that they refuse to sit tight.

*

A big head after the night before makes you wish the swallows would go someplace else and stay there.

*

The best sign of a person being tight is a loose tongue.

*

REMORSE: Another name for that dark-brown taste.

*

Many a drunk who thinks he's making a pass at an angel winds up holding the bag.

*

When some men come home to their wives half shot, they usually feel like finishing the job.

*

Drinking is one subject that has floored a lot of people.

*

Drinking would be less objectionable if it didn't make so many of us think that we can sing.

*

When a girl drinks like a fish, almost any old line will land her.

*

The toast of the evening isn't very crisp the next morning.

*

MORNING AFTER: When the getting up gets you down.

*

You can't fly with the owls at night and keep up with the eagles the next day.

*

INTOXICATION: Feeling sophisticated but not being able to pronounce it.

*

Drinking is bad. It was a hot sling that killed Goliath.

*

Seems only natural that Scotch whiskey should make you tight.

*

Thousands of lives have been destroyed by whiskey —but just look at all the boats that have been wrecked by water.

*

There wouldn't be half as many yes-men if there were no such expression as "Have another?"

*

You can lead some people to water, but why disappoint them?

*

BAR: A place where you start out fit as a fiddle and wind up tight as a drum.

*

Some folks try to get in touch with the spirit world through a medium. Most of us, though, use a bartender.

*

Many a man knows what his drinking limit is—but he gets drunk before he gets to it.

*

PRETZEL: A drinking man's filter.

*

Couples who are always lit seldom make a good match.

*

COCKTAIL PARTY: Where you say the worst things about your best friends.

*

The fellow with the real drinking problem is the one whose wife insists on accompanying him to the bar.

*

You can't keep in shape if you let yourself get tight in a loose joint.

*

Once a girl has an edge on, there's never a dull moment.

*

When a girl says she never drinks anything stronger than pop, maybe you'd better check up on what Pop drinks.

*

CHAMPAGNE HANGOVER: The wrath of grapes.

*

Our private opinion is that pleasure is like a hornet—it usually ends with a sting.

*

The fifth highball usually brings out the tipsy in you.

*

Whiskey improves with age. The older a man gets, the better he likes it.

*

According to a chemist, alcohol was first made in Arabia. That could explain some of those nights.

*

The size of the U.S. liquor bill indicates that a lot of us don't save for a rainy day, but for a wet night.

*

Sometimes an extra highball can put you behind the eight ball.

*

Buying a drink for the house is a good way to meet a lot of people you can live without.

*

BARTENDER: The only psychiatrist who works in an apron.

*

Guys who keep on getting lit ain't bright.

*

After an evening of drinking like a fish, many a man has found himself in the Sea of Matrimony.

*

No man who hasn't drunk liquor knows what a luxury cold water is.

*

Folks who say we spend more for alcohol than for education just don't realize the things you can learn at a drinking party.

*

Many a fellow who starts out with a bottle ends up in the can.

*

There was a time when, if a girl took two drinks, she went out like a light. But times have changed! Some of our modern girls take two drinks and out goes the light.

*

After an evening of drinking, some girls get weak in the nays.

*

Paying alimony is like tipping a barber for conversation you didn't want; but for the woman it's a guaranteed annual wage.

*

Marriage is supposed to be a give-and-take proposition, which to a number of men is a lot of boloney—especially when he has to give and she takes all she can get.

*

ALIMONY: A man's best proof that he has to pay for his mistakes, or, the installment method of paying for experience.

*

Girls are no longer marrying for better or worse—they're marrying for more or less. And the guys begin the sharing o' the green.

*

In these days of so many divorces, it seems that most of the "courting" is done after marriage.

*

Paying alimony is like having the TV set on after you've fallen asleep, or paying the installments on a wrecked car.

*

After a woman takes the shirt off your back she looks for somebody who dresses better than you do. After all, you know, alimony is matrimonial insurance for women paid by men for having poor judgment.

*

ALIMONY: A matter of paying on time for something you'll never get. For instance, like taxation without representation.

*

Why is it that so many women will tell the judge their husbands aren't worth a dime, but will still plead for big fat alimony checks?

*

Would you say a couple could be considered compatible these days if they agree on the size of the alimony?

*

Some fellows claim they shouldn't be forced to pay alimony, because they committed matrimony while in a state of temporary insanity.

*

From the looks of things, seems like some women begin to figure on alimony before the honeymoon is over.

*

Ever notice that most of the battles of the sexes are over alimony?

*

Adoration, separation and reparation.

*

Alimony has one advantage. A husband no longer has to bring his paycheck home to his wife—he can mail it to her.

*

With the heavy alimony they pay out, it's easy to see why the girls find their former husbands have "ex-appeal."

*

Because of the alimony laws, marriage is the only business that pays money to one of its partners after it fails.

*

SONG TITLE: "Alimony every week reminds me I was wrong."

*

How come a woman will treat her husband like thirty cents, and then demand thousands when another woman gets him?

*

ALIMONY: When a poor sap goes from a costarring spot to a supporting role; it changes a rich man into a poor bachelor.

*

Until a man can get alimony by crossing his legs and showing his garters to a judge and jury, equal rights for men and women are only a snare and a delusion.

*

ALIMONY: The prize money in a divorce contest.

*

A fellow never knows the value of a woman's affections until she sues him; then he begins to realize it's a matter of wife and debt.

*

Some men never realize what their wives are worth until the judge sets the alimony payments. Then the poor fellow is forced to agree because it's the supporting thing to do.

*

ALIMONY: A man's cash surrender value; a contraction of the three words "all his money."

*

No matter how many times a woman is married abroad, she always comes back to America for her alimony.

*

A first mate is the one whose alimony keeps a guy broke. But to her it's heart-earned money.

*

ALIMONY: The method some women use for taking the drudgery out of housework; and many a man is forced to pay for his loved once.

*

A woman's tear-filled eyes and her quivering lips can make an old skinflint judge mighty generous with a man's bank account.

*

Before they were married the guy remembers thinking what a dear little thing she was—and as he sits there making out his alimony check he finds himself thinking the same thing.

*

ALIMONY: When husbands who were bounced have to send checks that are good.

*

Looks like the big payoff is the toll a man pays for taking the wrong turn in Lovers' Lane.

*

These days an unhappy marriage is one in which the woman doesn't get as much alimony as she expected.

*

ALIMONY: When the bride continues to get wedding gifts after the divorce.

*

Any husband seeking advice concerning the possibility of divorce should consult a man who is splitting his income between alimony and a second wife.

*

Of all the expensive hobbies, the collection of wives is the most expensive.

*

Paying alimony is like paying for a subscription to a magazine that is no longer published.

*

The word "alimony" comes from the Latin *alimonia*, which means nourishment. To the guy who is paying it, it means the high cost of guessing wrong.

*

Our advice to the girls is this: Meditate well before you make the final decision. Remember, alimony is next to worthless on a cold night.

*

Some fellows owe everything to their wives—and the gals are still collecting.

*

Might as well face it, men! More and more women are becoming wealthy by decrees in the divorce courts.

*

Many a man who isn't worth a cent is paying alimony because of a bad investment.

*

If any woman asks for alimony from her husband on the grounds that he gives her the hives, you can take it for granted that she is trying to put the bee on him.

*

Almost anyone can avoid paying alimony by developing his staying power. Either stay single or stay married.

*

Alimony is just like a kiss at a charity ball. It's all clear profit to the woman.

*

Thanks to Social Security, a man can be financially independent at sixty-five. Thanks to alimony, a woman can do the same thing at twenty-five.

*

Some women consider their husbands worthless, but their lawyers think otherwise.

*

United we stand, but divided somebody gets hooked for alimony.

*

Alimony is the fee a woman charges for name dropping.

*

Some of our politicians raise their voices and cry, "There is no tax on liberty!" It's obvious these fellows never heard of alimony.

*

Many a woman has solved her financial problem by exchanging her wedding gown for a divorce suit.

*

A grass widow is a woman who feels like a new man.

*

In Borneo, a man's wealth is measured by the number of wives he has. In America, it's how many wives he's paying alimony to.

*

Some women ask for very little when they divorce their husbands, and it's usually just one thing: the custody of his money.

*

There was a time in the old days when women married men for their money. Today they divorce them for it.

*

It takes a good round sum to square things with a lot of the girls.

*

Alimony is giving comfort to the enemy and a splitting headache to the guy who has to fork over.

*

Thanks to the judges' providence of modern women's needs,
Grass widows bloom in clover more often than in weeds.

*

ALIMONY: The fee for untying the knot that cost only a couple of bucks to tie; a fine levied on a man guilty of matrimony.

*

ANNIVERSARIES

Any time a wife delivers a "state of the union" speech you can be pretty darn sure that someone forgot a wedding anniversary present.

*

In celebrating wedding anniversaries, it is advisable that guests refrain from relating their marital troubles. The celebrating couple have enough of their own.

*

Today's my anniversary! I've been broke for —————— years.

*

There's one good thing about a man buying his wife an anniversary present. He doesn't have to forget it for another whole year.

*

It's a tribute to a husband's forgiving nature that he forgets the wedding anniversary—because painful memories are not so easily erased.

*

The best way a husband can surprise his wife with an anniversary gift is to give her just what she wanted.

*

Long after a man has forgotten his reasons for getting married, his wife always expects him to remember the date she lowered the boom.

*

STALEMATE: A husband who forgets his wedding anniversary.

*

Why is it that a woman won't let a man forget the anniversary of a wedding that happened so many years ago, but still can't recall how she dented the fender of the car only yesterday?

*

Instead of being angry when her husband forgets their wedding anniversary, the modern wife should be glad he doesn't forget that he's married.

*

Many a man who misses his anniversary catches it later.

*

When some couples celebrate their wedding anniversaries, it's merely the rest period between rounds.

*

Anniversary gifts help bring peace. So, in thinking of the future, fellows, don't forget the present.

*

When you are discouraged at times, just think of the others you might have married.

*

The biggest surprise the average husband can give his wife on their anniversary is to remember it.

*

When some couples celebrate their first wedding anniversary, it may actually be longer—depending on how long it took the girl to land him.

*

Wives: Want to know how to surprise your husband on your wedding anniversary? Simply mention the date.

*

All some husbands ask for in celebrating a wedding anniversary is two minutes of silence.

*

After a man has been married five years he celebrates his wooden anniversary; ten years his tin; fifteen years his crystal; twenty-five years his silver; fifty years his golden; seventy-five years his diamond. In other words, he's rewarded according to the suffering he has endured.

*

A wooden anniversary is the day on which a man realizes what a blockhead he was.

*

The silver wedding anniversary is the day on which
the couple celebrate the fact that the first twenty-five years
of their married life is finally over.

*

A thirty-fifth wedding anniversary is difficult to celebrate. It's too soon to brag and too late to complain.

*

The most impressive evidence of tolerance is a golden
wedding anniversary.

*

Henry Ford, when asked on his fiftieth wedding anniversary to give his formula for a successful married life,
replied that it was the same formula he had used to make
his automobile so successful: "Stick to one model."

*

Personally, we believe that a golden wedding anniversary is a wonderful occasion that should be met with
loud acclaim and cheers. After all, how often do you hear
of two people who can break all records for endurance and
live together as man and wife for fifty years?

*

Every so often we read in the papers that some man
has worked for the same boss for fifty years. Then the two
of them celebrate their golden wedding anniversary.

*

Beauty

Many a girl with a Sunday face has Saturday-night ideas.

*

It's always nice to meet a girl who is as pretty as a picture—unless she turns out to be a talkie.

*

Beauty isn't everything, but it sure is nice to look at.

*

The cuter the number, the harder it is to get hers.

*

A thing of beauty is a joy—except when her clothing and cosmetic bills come due.

*

A thing of beauty can make a man ugly all day.

*

Many a thing of beauty becomes a jaw forever.

*

Things of beauty often shake up men who view them minus makeup.

*

A thing of beauty is a great expense.

*

If the girls' faces are their fortunes, as they tell us, then all we've got to say is that a lot of present-day beauties ought to be arrested for counterfeiting.

*

Never go by appearances. Many a girl who looks like a million dollars has a ten-cent disposition.

*

When a girl is told she's as pretty as a picture, it puts her in a nice frame of mind.

*

Today any girl can be as pretty as a picture—providing she's well painted.

*

Some girls are as pretty as a picture, but their frames are cracked.

*

When a girl is as pretty as a picture, almost any fellow would like to have her hanging around his apartment.

*

Women find it pretty tough on the budget to stay easy on the eyes.

*

Many a girl who is a vision during the evening is a sight the next morning.

*

A beautiful woman is a blessing to the soul, a paradise to the eyes and a curse to the purse.

*

A girl who is beautiful to look at may be hard to look after.

*

Thanks to cosmetics, many a woman of fifty who used to look like sixty now looks like a million.

*

Life sure can be a heck of a trial
If a girl isn't born with a decent dial.

*

Some women look as young and beautiful as ever—but it sure is hurting the old man's bankroll.

*

The prettier a girl's map is, the easier it is for her to go places.

*

Beauty is only a skin game after all.

*

Beauty, so we're told, comes from within, but most girls seem to believe that it never hurts to have a good start on the outside too.

*

Some of us fellows are criticized for looking at a beautiful girl while we're engaged or married to another, but what the heck—just because a fellow is on a diet is no sign he can't look at the menu.

*

Show me a man who doesn't turn around to look at a beautiful woman, and I'll show you a man walking with his wife.

*

Did you ever notice that a pretty face can cause an awful lot of ugly talk?

*

A man will go a long way to save his face, but a girl just goes to the drugstore.

*

A pretty girl may be like a melody, but it's the plain ones who keep their husbands singing, "Home, Sweet Home."

*

Girls who are charmless
Will find men quite harmless.

*

When a girl is pretty and knows it, she spoils it.

*

The next thing to being young and pretty is being old and rich.

*

Beware of the girl who admits she's beautiful.

*

No matter how much girls try to improve on Mother Nature, they're not kidding Father Time.

*

Some girls—and this you've got to admit—
Do exaggerate their charms quite a bit.

*

When the daylight of youth begins to fade, there's many a woman who resorts to artificial light.

*

With all the feminine "extras" that add to the beauty of the opposite sex, a fellow never knows what he's up against.

*

A girl's face may be her fortune, but it's usually one of those fortunes that are made early in the morning.

*

The trouble with girls who look like a million is that they're generally looking for it too.

*

A girl may be heavenly looking and still not be of much earthly use.

*

Girls: Be pretty if you can, witty if you must, but be agreeable even if it kills you.

*

A pretty girl may be like a melody, but after you marry her you have to face the music.

*

Beauty is only skin deep, but a lot of girls would give a lot for that kind of skin.

*

A lot of girls who think they're beautiful enough to need a bodyguard really need a body.

*

Girls fit to be eyed
Are soonest tied.

*

It's a rare girl who wears the same face during the day that she got up with in the morning.

*

Little dabs of powder and little dabs of paint
Make a lot of women look like what they ain't.

*

Some women are really beautiful! Their hair is like spun gold, their eyes are like limpid pools of water at dusk, and their lips— Boy! What a mess they make on the rim of a coffee cup!

*

When girls start fishing for men they'll try all sorts of artificial lures.

*

Beware of fresh paint on women or houses.

*

The average girl would rather have beauty than brains, because she knows the average man can see better than he can think.

*

A beautiful girl is much easier to look at than listen to—but then who listens?

*

Beware of the girl who is a knockout, because she is sure to have had some ring experience.

*

There is no torture a woman would not endure to enhance her beauty.

*

A beautiful girl is even more beautiful when she's laughing.

*

The easier a girl is to look at, the harder a man looks.

*

A beautiful girl is one who has what it takes—to take what a fellow has.

*

Sometimes those finely chiseled features belong to a chiseler.

*

Don't waste your breath to tell your queen she's beautiful, young fellow, for every girl I've ever seen thinks that before you tell her.

*

The line forms to the left at the cosmetic counters when girls want to make up for lost sleep.

*

Many a teen-age girl has inherited her mother's beauty —straight from the dressing table.

*

FACT: It is more difficult to support admiration than it is to excite it.

*

Some girls are a sight for sore eyes; others just a sight.

*

A heavenly shape and lips red-painted,
Help a girl to get acquainted.

*

When a girl has lips like cherries, eyes like olives, and cheeks like marshmallows, what a time for a guy to be on a diet!

*

Girls who wear too much makeup
Look human only when they wake up.

*

It's an advantage to be beautiful. A girl can get attention without even trying, but after the first five minutes she's on her own.

*

The way we figure, a girl, even though she's beautiful, should learn to cook. A beautiful face and figure is no excuse for heartburn three times a day.

*

Our private opinion is that a fellow should never marry a girl for her looks. That's like buying a house because the paint job looks good.

*

Some fellows who used to drink in the beauty of their girl friends now just drink.

*

When a girl looks pretty and sweet enough to eat, it's a wise man who doesn't give her the opportunity.

*

Beauty is only skin deep, but it's a valuable asset to a girl if she hasn't any sense.

*

God made women beautiful so man would love her—then He made her foolish so she would love men.

*

When a woman wants to make herself as beautiful as she can, she should never take the advice of another woman. The other girls are too jealous to be objective.

*

Beauty fades with the fleeting years—so it's a wise woman who holds onto her good nature.

*

FACT: Beauty is more the result of how a girl makes up her mind than of how she makes up her face.

*

A shapely and beautiful girl is like a three-ring circus—a guy doesn't know where to look first.

*

A visiting Frenchman once said that the American girl is nothing more than an animated doll. OK, fellows, let's all stand up and sing "Oh, You Beautiful Doll."

*

The girl who thinks her face is her fortune usually has an inflated head.

*

A girl may be beautiful and dumb, but she is never ignorant of the fact that she is beautiful.

*

There's nothing about this glamour business that won't wash off with a cloth.

*

When a woman's face is her fortune, her husband usually has the cosmetic bills to prove it.

*

Tell a girl she is beautiful and she will like it but still not be sure you are in earnest, but this you can believe: Tell her she is prettier than some girl she *knows* is beautiful and—brother!—you've got her.

*

Beauty, like opportunity, can knock twice—and some fellows have had two black eyes to prove it.

*

Nothing makes a man forget something fancy like something a little fancier.

*

How come every time we meet a beautiful, voluptuous girl, either she is married or we are?

*

When a girl is the toast of the town, all the men want a bite.

*

Women have their beauty secrets—and men have their secret beauties.

*

Most girls want to be the gleam in a man's eye and the green in a woman's.

*

Beauty is like a strawberry—soon out of season but exquisite while it lasts—and like the strawberry, it isn't perfect without a good deal of sugar.

*

Any girl with an hourglass figure need never worry about the minutes of the next meeting.

*

The best beauty preparation in the world is a good night's sleep.

*

A woman's beauty lasts as long as her disposition stays sweet.

*

There's nothing that will break up an interesting intellectual conversation quicker than the arrival of a beautiful girl.

*

Some girls glamour for attention.

*

BIRTHDAYS

Someone has said that women are not economical, but just show me a woman who will put more than twenty-six candles on her fortieth birthday cake.

*

The twenty longest years of a girl's life are between her second and thirty-fifth birthday.

*

The best way for a man to remember his wife's birthday is to forget it just once.

*

Every so often a number of women's birthday clubs suspend their meetings indefinitely. The reason? Most of the members don't plan to have any more birthdays for a while.

*

It's tough when men have to grow old alone. Some of their wives haven't had a birthday in years.

*

If you really want to know what your wife wants for her birthday, go take a peek at what she bought.

*

It's remarkable how some women keep their youth. The fact is, they absolutely insist upon it every birthday.

*

Never forget your wife's birthday—just forget which one it is.

*

Whenever you quit having birthdays, you're dead!

*

It's hard to pick out a birthday gift for a wife when you know exactly what she wants.

*

Most of us accumulate birthdays faster than we learn to act our age.

*

Dinner's defrosting, Mother is not.
Today is her birthday and Dad forgot.

*

To whom it may concern: Happy Birthday! You deserve it!

*

If you ask a man the date of his birth he tells you only the year; if you ask a woman, she never tells you more than the day.

*

A man has a choice. He can either consult his wife before he buys her a birthday present—or she'll charge it later.

*

When that dreadful time comes when a woman celebrates her fortieth birthday, it's like a rocket launching—the countdown really begins.

*

The burning of candles on a woman's birthday cake rarely sheds much light on anything—particularly her age.

*

If a wife wants to surprise her husband on his birthday, she can do so by telling him her real age—or letting him win an argument once in a while.

*

Birthday meditation: At twenty most folks feel they will never grow old; at thirty they think that maybe they won't; at forty they begin to wonder a bit, and at fifty they kind of feel they're getting up there a bit—especially after trying to stay up until after midnight and then having to drag themselves down to work at seven o'clock in the morning.

*

Women don't observe birthdays—they only preserve them.

*

Wonder if women put candles on their birthday cake to make light of their age?

*

Everyone else may forget your birthday but your insurance man will always remember—usually with a card that reads: "Congratulations, we won again! Better luck next time!"

*

Some mothers and daughters act as if they're hurrying to reach the joint thirtieth birthday—from opposite directions.

*

A birthday is simply out of one year and into another.

*

Forget my birthday. After all, it's much kinder not to send me a reminder.

*

Isn't it funny how easy it is to pick out the wrong sizes in birthday presents?

*

It's amazing when a brother and sister—twins—celebrate their birthday. He'll boast of fifty, she'll admit to thirty.

*

The smart wife is the one who will knit a pair of socks for her husband—and then give them to him just before *her* birthday.

*

It's surprising that some wives expect hubby to remember their birthday when they never look a day older.

*

Birthdays are feathers in the broad wings of time.

*

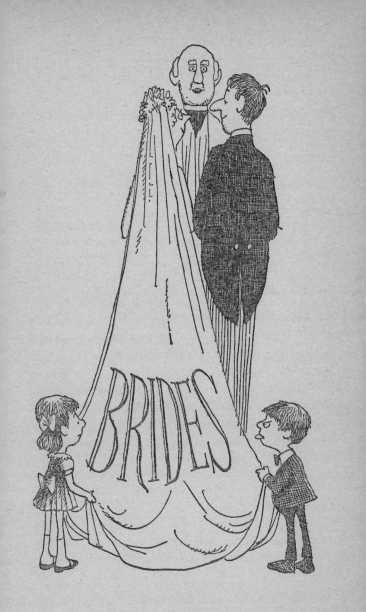

Brides: If you want things to run smoothly on the Sea of Matrimony, don't sail into him every time he's late for dinner.

*

The average bride is twenty—or precisely the number of years her father ages while paying her wedding bills.

*

Advice for a young bride will be found on top of a mayonnaise jar: "Keep cool, but don't freeze."

*

Being a bride is a hit-or-miss proposition. If she doesn't make a hit, she'll remain a miss.

*

Some brides, when saying, "I Do!" are probably wondering if they couldn't have done better.

*

There is nothing that rings a bell with a girl like wedding bells.

*

The only reason some brides promise to love, honor and obey is that they don't want to start an argument in front of all those people.

*

Many a bride, although given away, turns out to be a very expensive gift.

*

Just by putting a ring on her finger, many a man winds up under her thumb.

*

Modern brides are wearing their wedding dresses shorter—and oftener.

*

Cupid may be a good shot, but he sure makes some awful Mrs.

*

Women are always changing their minds, but did you ever hear of a bridegroom being left at the church?

*

If her bridegroom doesn't seem to possess the usual nine faults, no bride should be too discouraged. She'll probably discover after the wedding that he has enough to give the marriage plenty of zest.

*

Many a girl has married for mink only to discover later that what she really got was a skunk.

*

Every bride isn't happy—just triumphant.

*

BRIDE: The girl who quit playing ball with the boys after she made a good catch.

*

Judging from some of the specimens they pick for husbands, no wonder brides blush.

*

Something found out by brides of the past is that the second, third and fourth babies are not nearly as "breakable" as the first.

*

Why is it the bride always looks stunning, and the bridegroom stunned?

*

A bride going up the aisle to be married looks as confident as a man laying down four aces.

*

A bride never forgives a bridegroom who has to stifle a yawn during the wedding ceremony. He'll hear about it all the rest of his days.

*

The modern bride is a girl who puts her foot down as soon as her husband has carried her over the threshold.

*

A girl can sometimes talk a fellow into double harness, but she'll have a hard time keeping the "blinders" on him.

*

After hearing all this talk about beautiful brides, where do all the plain-looking wives come from?

*

Some girls have to work like a horse to get a groom.

*

Surprisingest of all surprises
Is a new bride's face when she arises.

*

It takes a lot of cooking to make a marriage pan out.

*

All it takes for a bride to be a good cook is confidence, patience and a lot of modern kitchen appliances.

*

One of the best solutions to a bride's poor cooking is bicarbonate of soda.

*

The first few home-cooked meals are hard on a bride's nerves—and on a groom's stomach.

*

There's one thing all brides would like—a cookbook with a happy ending.

*

A bride of eighteen faces the task of cooking fifty thousand meals. Better keep that can opener handy.

*

Don't neglect your cookery, gals. "Kissin' don't last but cookin' do."

*

The smart bride says the others can have the key to the city—just give her a good, reliable can opener.

*

It's mighty hard to keep a man's love warm without a kitchen stove.

*

The most effective perfume a bride can use is the odor of corned beef and cabbage.

*

Newlyweds soon discover that it takes a lot of juggling to balance the old family budget.

*

Politicians and bridegrooms have one thing in common—they both forget their campaign promises.

*

You'll soon learn that sometimes it's just as hard to find a husband after marriage as before.

*

The ABC's of a bride: Always Be Calm.

*

Bridal veils should always be saved. Later on they make wonderful mosquito netting for Junior's crib.

*

Isn't it nice to be married and not have to worry
where your next date is coming from?

*

A new marriage is something like a new house. It
takes time, and suffers a few cracks before it finally settles
down on its firm foundation.

*

Any girl who thinks marriage is the end of her education has a lot to learn.

*

If you don't believe in cooperation, just watch what
happens to a car when one wheel comes off.

*

There's trouble a-brewing when matrimony becomes
a matter-of-money.

*

Successful marriages are based on two books—the
cookbook and the checkbook.

*

It's a wise couple that uses cash down when feather-
ing their nest.

*

Don't allow ready tears to mildew your marriage.

*

You'll never really know your husband until the first
time you ask him for money.

*

Remember that marriage is a game of give and take—
if he doesn't give you enough, take it.

*

With *his* credit cards and *your* charge accounts, you
shouldn't have a money problem.

*

The sensibly married give constant attention to the
state of the union.

*

Housework is one thing there's no catching up with. You go to bed at night with everything done, but while you're sleeping the sheets are getting wrinkled, dust is settling and stomachs are getting empty.

*

After meeting most of your in-laws, don't you think you were a little mistaken in not believing the theory of evolution?

*

The bride's big problem is making the "bud" in budget blossom into a flower of security.

*

Always come to the breakfast table looking your very best, because the first morning you don't the newsboy may be late with the morning paper.

*

Belittling the person to whom you are married is belittling the person who is belittling.

*

The first year of married life is the "formative period," and the only year a husband can be trained to put on an apron.

*

The one word above all others that makes marriage a success is "ours."

*

A marriage certificate is a legal paper that lets you girls keep the game in captivity after the hunting season is over.

*

After a young couple get married, one of their biggest expenses for several years is disproving unrealistic theories which they have picked up from advertisements, casual conversations and daydreams.

*

The trouble with children today is that they are just as thoughtless, selfish, lazy, irresponsible, silly and reckless as were the preceding generations.

*

Saying yes to a child is like blowing up a balloon—you have to know when to stop.

*

Research shows that youngsters mature faster today than they did a few years ago. By the time they recover from mumps, measles, chicken pox and other childhood ailments, they break out with puppy love.

*

Raising a bunch of youngsters is the biggest heir-conditioning job ever undertaken.

*

This you can believe: When a youngster hears a bad word, it goes in one ear—and out of his mouth.

*

Kids never change. First they won't hang up their clothes—then they won't hang up the phone.

*

You can usually account for a child before it comes, but once it's here—good Lord!

*

There's one thing to be said in favor of our youngsters: They never pull out pictures of their grandparents.

*

The loudest noise on the face of the earth is one youngster telling another to shut up.

*

Why is it that children speak so doggone distinctly when they say something they shouldn't?

*

Pity the poor kids! They have to go to bed when they're not sleepy and get up when they are.

*

A problem child is one who puts two and two together and gets curious.

*

Although children are deductible, they can also be very taxing.

*

The weather and kids run true to form.
There's always that lull before the storm.

*

Heredity is what makes the mother and father wonder a little about each other.

*

If a child is spoiled, it's probably because you can't spank two grandmothers.

*

Whenever a modern child takes no for an answer, you can bet he asked a pretty shifty question.

*

One thing about raising kids is that they'll grow up in almost any kind of dirt.

*

Mothers can buy a rugged youngster a brand-new pair of socks—and a week later find they're not worth a darn.

*

The more children a couple have, the less likely they are to have modern decorating schemes.

*

I suspect the secret of raising a child properly is knowing when to give it a big hand—and where.

*

What you don't know takes a heck of a lot of explaining to our modern youngsters.

*

Have you noticed how quickly the youngsters grow up these days? No sooner do the parents get through sitting up *with* them than they start sitting up *for* them.

*

For adult education, there's nothing beats a flock of kids.

*

Your children are growing up when the boys want to stop going out with the girls, preferring to stay home with them.

*

Among the things that seem to grow by leaps and bounds, the kids overhead top the list of those who live in the apartment below.

*

Thoughtful children do not call for a drink as soon as they go to bed. They wait until their parents have gone too.

*

Any child who is raised strictly by the book is probably a first edition.

*

You can tell a child is growing up when he stops asking where he came from and starts refusing to tell you where he's going.

*

Children are those who get you down during the day —and up at night.

*

When children ask awkward questions, invention is the necessity of mother.

*

Even children with perfect table manners will spill the beans now and then.

*

A child's ear is that delicate auditory instrument that can't hear a parent's bellow from the next room but picks up the faintest far-off tinkle of an ice-cream cart.

*

Children are unpredictable—you never know what the neighbors will learn next.

*

About the only two things a child will share willingly are communicable diseases and his mother's age.

*

Nothing makes food go farther than trying to feed an active toddler.

*

It's rough being a youngster. If he's noisy he gets a licking, and if he's quiet he gets castor oil.

*

No one minds little pitchers having big ears as long as they don't spill anything.

*

A lot of mothers are inclined to believe it would be much wiser to give themselves the vitamins, and the kids the tranquilizers.

*

Two of anything but children make a pair; two of them make a mob.

*

No two children are alike—particularly if one is yours and the other one isn't.

*

With children, the better the meal, the shorter the blessing.

*

Nothing makes a child worse than belonging to a neighbor.

*

Children haven't changed much in the last forty years or so—and that's what worries a lot of parents.

*

The trouble with having outspoken kids is that the parents are frequently left holding the bag the youngsters let the cat out of.

*

Children are the only people on the face of the earth who can change a mother-in-law's name from "Hey You!" to "Grandma."

*

The trouble with most children is that when they're not being a lump in the throat, they're being a pain in the neck.

*

Children can bring much happiness into a home, but what we usually get is a bunch of stray dogs, cats and the like.

*

The problem for many a child is whether to waste time discussing a request with dad, or wait until mom gets home and take it straight to the summit.

*

Most children are descended from a long line their mothers once listened to.

*

You've got to face it—out of the mouths of babes come words we shouldn't have said in the first place.

*

Children are at a perfect age when they're too old to cry at night and too young to ask for the car.

*

One of life's most pleasant times is when the youngsters get to the age where parents don't have to pretend any longer that they know everything.

*

Children may tear up a house, but they never break up a home.

*

The home life of a lot of youngsters is all tied up in a series of "nots."

*

Children say the funniest things—and usually in front of the wrongest people.

*

The danger is not in the big ears of little pitchers, but in the big mouths.

*

Children are a real comfort in your old age—and they make you reach it sooner too.

*

Children are natural mimics. They act like their parents in spite of every effort to teach them good manners.

*

There's nothing like children to keep a family together—especially when you can't get a baby-sitter.

*

Did you ever notice how those little "lambs" can pull the wool over their parents' eyes?

*

Why is it that children who eat safety pins always seem to prefer the open ones?

*

CREDIT and CREDIT CARDS

Many a man gets credit for having push when all he had was pull.

*

A lot of fellows get credit for being self-made when they merely used their wives' judgment.

*

Some folks are given credit for being good when they're only growing old.

*

When it comes to owning big cars, beautiful fur coats, diamonds and other jewelry, you've got to give the American public credit.

*

A charge account is what a wife uses to display confidence in her husband. Or to keep him from becoming too independent.

*

Nobody looks into a fellow's credit status when he goes to borrow trouble.

*

If a lot of us were credited with what we know, and charged with what we think we know—boy!—wouldn't we be in the red, though?

*

FACT: If you don't claim too much intelligence, folks will give you credit for more than you have.

*

When you show folks a few "bucks," they'll give you credit for having sense.

*

Credit, like dope, when used to excess, leads to the gutter.

*

Edward Bellamy, nineteenth-century author of *Looking Backward,* predicted that in a hundred years or so people would no longer use cash at all. Every year he seems closer to the truth.

*

Much good can be done if you're not too critical of who gets the credit.

*

A large number of people are trying to keep up with the Joneses—and a number of creditors are trying to catch up with them.

*

The woman who hasn't a thing to wear must be married to that rare man to whom no one will give credit.

*

You can get anything you want on credit these days —except money.

*

Some of us get credit for being patient, when actually we haven't the nerve to start anything.

*

It's foolish for anyone to buy a pair of shoes on credit —if he has to wear them out running from bill collectors.

*

The quickest way to lose your shirt is to put too much on the cuff.

*

CREDIT: A device that enables you to start at the bottom—and go into the hole.

*

The hog you buy on credit will grunt until it's paid for.

*

Some folks pay their dues when due, some when overdue, some never do. How do you do?

*

The surest way of establishing your credit is to work so hard that you won't need it.

*

It's a man's own fault if, every time the ghost walks on payday, his creditors are on hand to haunt him.

*

If you give a woman credit for anything, she'll take it.

*

Creditors have better memories than debtors.

*

Lots of folks get credit for being cheerful, when they're just proud of their teeth.

*

Some fellows give their wives a lot of credit, but the cautious ones give theirs cash.

*

In these days there are the haves, the have-nots and the charge-its.

*

A lot of people these days use sign language. They sign for this and sign for that.

*

The only time we don't get credit for what we do is when we look to the wrong source for it.

*

Most any department store is willing to give a wife credit for what her husband earns.

*

The average American is too proud to steal, too proud to beg and too poor to pay cash. That's why we give him credit.

*

You can trust some people to the ends of the earth— and others not until they get there.

*

CREDIT CARD: A convenient way to spend money you wish you had.

*

Someone once said that a credit card is a device that keeps a man from having cash in his pockets. Well, maybe so, but the first device of that kind was a wife.

*

Most of us wouldn't have such fat wallets if we'd re-move our credit cards.

*

In our credit-card civilization, the man who pays cash must feel as though everyone has him under suspicion as a fleeing embezzler.

*

Even with a pocketful of credit cards, a fellow still needs to carry a little loose change on him to feed the parking meters.

*

FACT: The pioneers who crossed the wild and un-tamed wilderness, fighting and paying their way as they went, now have descendants who won't even drive to town without a credit card.

*

There is nothing that will raise your standard of liv-ing quicker than a credit card—for a month or so.

*

Eat, drink and be merry, for tomorrow you may lose your credit card.

*

CREDIT CARD: The sweet buy and buy.

*

At least credit cards have put an end to one practice —that of a wife going through her husband's pocket for money.

*

Life has many ups and downs,
Ofttimes changing our smiles to frowns.
But one of the blows that hits real hard
Is the loss of our favorite credit card.

*

The credit card has created another American first—instant debt.

*

The fellow who doesn't know where his next dollar is coming from usually has a credit card to show where it will go.

*

I'll tell you something even handier than a credit card. It eliminates waiting, ends billing and is honored everywhere. It's called money.

*

Many a man is poor today because his credit card was good yesterday.

*

Credit cards have ruined more men than blondes.

*

Remember before credit cards became popular? No one had to wait until the end of the month to find out how broke he was.

*

Money isn't everything—but a credit card almost is.

*

There was a time when folks had what they called a promissory note. Today it's called a credit card.

*

It may be true that you can't buy happiness with money—but you still can do a pretty good job of it with a credit card.

*

What this country really needs is a credit card for taxpayers.

*

Some of us carry so many credit cards we don't bother to open our wallet—we just shuffle it.

*

Some fellows have found a new kind of togetherness. After they give their wives a credit card, they won't let her out of their sight.

*

Did you ever know anyone who used to conveniently forget his wallet? Well, he's changed! Now he forgets his credit card.

*

The way we figure, a man can have so many credit cards that he could be bankrupt for six months before he knew about it.

*

Most folks manage to keep in pretty fair touch with reality—while on the other hand there are millions of credit-card users.

*

Love once made the world go round; now credit cards do the job.

*

Mom sure gets a big charge out of Dad's credit cards.

*

CREDIT CARDS: Due unto others.

*

With all the credit cards in existence, would you say we are living in IOUtopia?

*

It's bad enough to live beyond our income, but a lot of us have recently discovered that we're living beyond our credit cards.

*

DENTISTS

The human mind may not be able to imagine how long eternity is, but if you've ever waited for a dentist to pull a tooth, you have a fair idea.

*

The thing that makes going to the dentist so tough is preparing for that long hard grind.

*

Our personal opinion is that a dentist is a prestidigitator who, while putting metal in your mouth, pulls coins out of your pocket.

*

CAVITY: An empty space ready to be stuffed with dental bills.

*

It wasn't too many years ago that dentists charged a *flat* fee for cleaning teeth, X rays, extractions and the like, but somehow or other, during recent years these tooth technicians have sort of knocked the *l* out of flat.

*

There's no apprehension like waiting in a dentist's office. And no happiness like finding out it didn't hurt after all.

*

I once read that a psychologist said dentists should tell jokes to their patients. Well, most of them do, their favorite being: "Now this isn't going to hurt a bit."

*

The next time you go to the dentist and are worried about it, try double parking. Then you'll have something to keep your mind off the pain.

*

Never argue with your dentist—it may result in bad fillings.

*

Dentists can often make a toothache go away by merely saying two magic words: "You're next."

*

A scientist once said the teeth of a gorilla are so deeply set that they can't be pulled. Maybe so, but we've got an idea this scientist doesn't know our dentist.

*

The most enjoyable way to see your dentist is to meet him in the neighborhood tavern.

*

A dentist is the only fellow I can think of offhand who actually prefers the company of a man with a hole in his head.

*

DENTIST: The only fellow who can tell a woman to shut her mouth and get away with it.

*

To increase the value of gold, have it handled by your dentist.

*

When some folks sit in a dentist's chair you never hear a whimper out of them—just yelling and screaming.

*

When a dentist returns from a vacation, it's usually right back to the old grind.

*

For lack of anything else to say, some dentists just bore you to death.

*

Girls who are looking for a man whose slightest touch will make them tremble all over will do well to see their dentist.

*

Strange, but it's when you have the nerve that you're afraid to go to the dentist.

*

If you insist on looking down in the mouth, take up dentistry.

*

QUESTION: Is there any longer time in the world than the ten minutes you're sitting in a dentist's chair, mouth crammed, waiting for a crown to set?

*

One sure way to make time fly is to have a weekly appointment with your dentist.

*

Some pains, like knives, give folks distraction, but an aching tooth drives them to extraction.

*

Only a dentist can make a living on the nerve of some people.

*

Some dentists use the word "remove" instead of "extract," but getting Junior to the dentist is still like pulling teeth.

*

You can't win with a dentist! Any time you have a tussle with one, the best you can wind up with is a draw.

*

Some dentists claim that slightly protruding teeth make a girl more beautiful. Could be, and they're a great help too in eating corn on the cob.

*

Did you ever get the feeling, while your dentist was probing around among your molars, that he had missed his calling and was intended to be a deep-sea diver instead?

*

Wonder if the study of teeth is referred to as odontology because of the frequency with which dental patients holler, "Oh, don't!"

*

DENTIST'S OFFICE: A chamber of hollers.

*

Most dentists take a stand against useless tooth pulling. In other words, it gives patients a chance to get their fill.

*

*I'll bet it would make any mortal grin and laugh away
    his care
If he could see his dentist sit in another dentist's chair.*

*

DENTIST: A man who works for his own teeth by taking out those of others.

*

There's one thing in favor of a dentist appointment. It's an excuse which permits you to have the afternoon off without deduction from sick leave or vacation.

*

PUZZLEMENT: Do dentists really expect an answer when they ask a question after filling your mouth with instruments?

*

Wouldn't it be wonderful to be a dentist for just one day, and be able to tell your wife to open and shut her mouth as *you* pleased?

*

Personally, my objection to going to the dentist is that after I'm seated, he grabs something that resembles a crochet needle with a red-hot stinger on the end of it and jabs it down my tooth to the point about opposite where my suspenders fork in the back.

*

*It's easy enough to be happy when life is a bright and
  rosy wreath,
But the man worthwhile is the one who can smile while
  the dentist is filling his teeth.*

*

Outside of those newfangled bent-pipe deals, just about the most uncomfortable chairs I can think of are the dentist's and the electric.

*

I wonder if the world will ever have permanent peace or painless dentistry?

*

DENTIST: He'll give you the drill of your life.

*

Our private opinion is that the happiest time in anyone's life is the first twenty minutes after an aching tooth has been pulled.

*

Dentists tell us that husbands lose fewer teeth than wives do, and they should know. Maybe it's because the old man has less chance to open his mouth, eh?

*

Nothing prompts the payment of an old dental bill like a new toothache.

*

The worst thing about having a dentist clean your teeth is having to spoil the job by eating so soon afterward.

*

FACT: Married men show much less fear of going to the dentist than single men do. I suspect the reason is that the dentist keeps telling him to open his mouth instead of to shut it.

*

How come when a dentist is drilling
On a tooth that needs filling
He keeps up a chatter
As though nothing's the matter?
And there we are with a mouth full of tools—no chance to talk,
No chance to squawk.
All we can do is just sit there and listen to the drill hum
—And nearly go nuts when it strikes the gum.

*

An example of nonchalance is a dentist who whistles while he works.

*

A dentist is a strange type of fellow who is found in the east, west, north and south—and who is happiest when he's down in the mouth.

*

All I can say about dentists who fill you with their incessant chatter is that I'm *bored* with their conversation.

*

Wonder if it's reality or something purely mental
That makes our teeth start aching when we hear the word "dental"?

*

The way we figure, a dentist always feels in the pink when he's poking his fingers around some gorgeous girl's gums.

*

When an irresistible force meets an immovable body, a good lawyer can put the skids under both and marriage becomes an institution that's lost two more of its inmates.

*

A lot of separations are caused by illness. They both got sick of each other.

*

Check on the number of divorces in and around your community and you'll have to admit there's a lot of split decisions going on these days.

*

One judge called marriage a lottery. That's the trouble with it—too many people want another chance.

*

The old-fashioned girls preserved fruit; the modern ones can their husbands.

*

It's just no use trying to make a girl eat out of your hand when she's all fed up.

*

The high divorce rate merely indicates that the modern girl can't make up her mind whether she wants a man for a hubby or a hobby.

*

Her sweetie may have been the berries, but now she's giving him the razz.

*

If marriages are made in heaven, a new shipping clerk is needed up there—one who won't get the wrong addresses on so many of them.

*

Divorce suits clothe lawyers with the legal right to take their clients to the cleaners.

*

Some women who are on the verge of getting a divorce hesitate, deciding to kick the subject around a while.

*

DIVORCE: A condition brought on by two people who were crazy to get married.

*

Long engagements are the only really effective way of staving off divorces. If they're long enough, that is.

*

Some folks consult a masseur or a chiropractor when they want to get rid of a pain in the neck. Others get a divorce.

*

Judging by the birth and divorce statistics, people today don't multiply as the folks of old did, but they sure do divide faster.

*

The picture from start to finish amounts to this: Infatuated, consolidated, mismated, expostulated, agitated, litigated, compensated, liberated. . . . Next?

*

It's a doggone short step from hugging to slugging.

*

With so many divorcées around the country, it's hard to tell who's whose.

*

In the old days marriage used to be a sacred contract. Today it's more like a ninety-day option.

*

Many a man's goose has been cooked by his wife's getting steamed up.

*

As soon as a girl gets her divorce, she gets back her maiden aim—to get a new louse on life.

*

Easy divorces have just about put arguing out of business.

*

Some men get married because they're sick and tired of eating in restaurants; others gets a divorce for the same reason.

*

Lots of divorces are caused by men who marry to get a home—and then stay away from it.

*

A pastor once said that marriage is like a sweet song. Could be, but too often one party gives the other the air.

*

Judging by the divorce rate, a lot of couples who say, "I do," don't.

*

Many an explosion has been caused by the appearance of an old flame.

*

Believe it or not, there's nothing colder than an old flame that's burned out.

*

RENO: Where people go to kick the marriage habit.

*

The man who regularly wears overalls seldom appears in a divorce suit.

*

Insanity is grounds for divorce in some states, but grounds for marriage in all.

*

If marriages are made in heaven, they must be breaking in new help.

*

She used to be his heart's delight, but now she's the light that failed.

*

DIVORCE: A sure method of getting rid of a mother-in-law.

*

At first he claimed he knew her like a book, but now he wants to put her on the shelf.

*

According to a doctor, shock will restore a man's speech. So will a divorce.

*

A lot of divorces are merely antitrust suits.

*

Divorce has become so common that some folks are staying married just to be different.

*

Lawyers are paid better for getting folks a divorce than ministers were for marrying them. But then the ministers didn't have to dig up a lot of evidence.

*

The bone of contention with some folks is often a meaty blonde.

*

RENO: A large inland seaport in America with the tide running in and the untied running out.

*

If the world is going to the dogs, it's because everyone has a bone to pick.

*

Seems like the time is fast approaching when the number of divorces will equal the number of marriages, which proves that love is finding a way—out!

*

In these days a couple marry, and the first thing you know, they have a little divorce.

*

Maybe if the divorce courts didn't separate some couples, the police would have to.

*

A divorcée has one advantage over other women. She can give references.

*

There's one thing to be said in favor of divorces—they sure do keep a lot of marriageable men in circulation.

*

GRASS WIDOW: The angel a man once loved, the human being he married, and the devil he divorced.

*

When love jells, the result is usually a jam.

*

Sometimes it costs a guy big money to have a small change of heart.

*

With so many divorces these days, more parents are running away from home than kids.

*

Many a marriage tie is cut by a blonde's sharp figure.

*

The split-up is usually caused by a great mental something-or-other and intensive whatchamacallit.

*

Many a marriage turns into a triangle because someone didn't know where to draw the line.

*

The ever-rising divorce rate is proof of man's never-ending search for a lasting peace.

*

Forbidden fruit is often responsible for many a bad jam.

*

Life is funny. A girl marries a man because his muscles rippled so beautifully when he went swimming—then she divorces him because he spends more time in the bedroom doing setting-up exercises than anything else.

*

Ever notice how peaceful bird housekeeping is? Penthouse orioles never mate with reed-nesting blue jays.

*

One reason some marriages fail is because the wife and her husband are in love with the same woman.

*

RENO: A great spot for getting rid of stalemates.

*

Some of the girls wish they could divorce the guy without making him happy.

*

Some of the men who married to escape the fighting are now getting divorced for the same reason.

*

Problems in marriage are often caused by a man showing his worst side to his better half.

*

Grass widows today aren't as they were in the old days. They're still grass widows, but they certainly aren't green.

*

Matches are made in heaven, burst into flame at Niagara Falls and are extinguished in Reno.

*

Lawyers are at the bottom of a lot of divorces, but they succeed in coming out on top.

*

We often wonder what stirs up these emotional ill winds that blow the matrimonial ships on the rocks. Maybe it's because when a girl finds a man she thinks is just what the doctor ordered, she later discovers the guy is just a pill.

*

You know it's a fact that it takes horse sense and stable thinking to stay hitched these days.

*

As the scraps accumulate, a hash is made of marriage.

*

The ironic observation of Salacrou, the French playwright, is worth remembering: "Divorce is quite useless. One gets married for lack of judgment. Then one gets divorced for lack of patience. And finally one remarries for lack of memory!"

*

The wife who hunts for the woman responsible for alienating her husband's affections may find her by looking in the mirror.

*

RENO: The city of otherly love.

*

A lot of dirt is dug up in the grounds for divorce.

*

Some folks have been married and divorced so many times you'd think they were a sucker for a parlay.

*

Some "better halves" become "bitter seconds."

*

Before marriage it used to be: "Let me call you sweetheart, I'm in love with you." Later on it's: "Now let me tell you something, baby, I'm fed up."

*

Some gals have been to Reno so many times they're actually swap-worn.

*

DIVORCE: A legal procedure that usually precedes a fashionable wedding.

*

A lot of divorce-court triangles are made with curves.

*

Many marriages crack up when the creditors crack down. In fact, the new version of the modern triangle is: the husband, the wife and the loan company.

*

Seems like people nowadays get married before they know each other—and get divorced when they do.

*

Marriages may be made in heaven but the separation usually occurs when the principals come down to earth.

*

Did it ever dawn on you that in a lot of cases marriage ends the way it began—with people throwing things?

*

FRIENDLY DIVORCE: She got the dog and he got the doghouse.

*

It's getting so the old familiar greeting of "How's your wife?" is being changed to "Who's your wife?"

*

Divorces come so easy these days that women don't even cry at weddings anymore.

*

I suspect the reason Cupid makes so many bad shots is that he is shooting at the heart while looking at a pair of well-filled stockings.

*

DIVORCE: A decision by an umpire who didn't see the game.

*

Many a fellow's clinging vine turns out to be poison ivy.

*

When a wife keeps the old man in hot water, it usually dissolves the union.

*

Some fellows want a divorce right after their "mirage."

*

A thing of beauty is a joy—until she sees a lawyer.

*

Some women get even with their husbands by staying married to them.

*

Some fellows want to divorce their wives because the gals haven't spoken to them in weeks. Better think twice, fellows; wives like that are hard to find.

*

Fewer marriages would skid
If more who say, "I do," did!

*

One of the reasons we have divorce courts is that husbands who promised they would die for their wives haven't come through.

*

There's many a man who leaves his wife on account of another woman—her mother.

*

The divorce rate won't be quite so high when women learn that the reason a man loves a dog is because the dog worships him.

*

Love is a quest; a proposal a request; marriage is a conquest; and the divorce, that's the inquest.

*

Most divorces are based on incompatability, or at least the first two syllables of the word.

*

Some couples marry in haste and repent at Reno.

*

Many a woman goes to Reno to get de-bossed.

*

MODERN DIVORCE: She keeps everything but her husband.

*

Court statistics show that wives get 65 percent of the divorces. It may be noted, also that they get 100 percent of the alimony.

*

A "hot number" is something that a man plays around with—and his wife burns.

*

Many a "go-getter" is sorry after he got her.

*

Most men can't afford to divorce their wives in the style to which they've become accustomed.

*

Fewer people would have trouble with their wedlock of they'd remember the combination.

*

There's often only one thing wrong with wedlock—the lock wore out too fast.

*

People wouldn't get divorced for such trivial reasons if they didn't get married for such trivial reasons.

*

Any fellow who thinks he chose a bad mate can always appease himself if he realizes how much worse it could have been if he had married his mother-in-law.

*

It's been said that marriage is the highway to heaven. If that's true, there sure are a lot of folks who are on a detour.

*

An old flame can make it pretty hot.

*

When a marriage gives out it's often because there hasn't been enough give in.

*

You may not believe it but a man doubled up with pain is sometimes cured by a divorce.

*

I suspect that one way to reduce the number of divorces would be to have people do their courting wearing their everyday clothes.

*

A lot of marriage ties are severed by a sharp tongue.

*

It's much easier to fall in love than to wiggle out of it.

*

RENO: Where the honeymoon express is finally uncoupled.

*

If it suits her purpose, certain women can shed a man as easily and as naturally as a rattlesnake can shed its skin.

*

Judging from the divorce rate, a lot of lovesickness these days is strictly psychoromantic.

*

A trip to Reno is for the purpose of name-dropping.

*

A lot of divorces are caused by a fellow's thinking he is footloose and family-free.

*

There was a time when a man bragged about one wife and four kids. Today men brag about four wives and one kid.

*

Divorce puts the *mar* in marriage.

*

When a couple get a divorce, they can divide everything except their memories.

*

Many a matrimonial cruise has been shipwrecked because a button got caught on a foreign permanent wave.

*

Looks like it's about as risky to lend your name as your money these days.

*

Divorce statistics seem to prove that this is the age of flight.

*

Family Life

The average family consists of a husband who makes money, and a wife and kids who make it necessary.

*

Having a big family around is a good way to make sure there'll always be someone to answer the phone—and forget the message.

*

The night shift in most families is the gang that takes out of the refrigerator what the day shift puts in.

*

It was Tolstoi who said: "The modern family is like a tiny little boat sailing in a storm on a vast ocean. It can keep afloat if it is ruled by one will. But when those in the boat begin struggling, the boat is upset."

*

Happy words in a family multiply like guinea pigs.

*

The right temperature at home is maintained by warm hearts, not hot heads.

*

Universal peace sounds ridiculous to the head of the average family.

*

Families are groups of people no two of whom like their breakfast eggs cooked the same way.

*

One advantage of a large family is that staying up with the baby is a good excuse for waiting up until the teen-agers are safely home.

*

Why is it that people always come to the back door when the sink is full of dirty dishes?

*

Most families do not feel it contributes to gracious living to have whine at every meal.

*

No matter what a man may be doing around the house on his day off, his wife can always think up something that is far more important than what he is doing.

*

The best way to tell who's boss in the family is to listen to the husband and then watch the wife.

*

The most prominent feature of many a modern family is wall-to-wall carping.

*

Keeping peace in a large family requires patience, love, understanding, and at least two television sets.

*

A good family circle is best maintained by permitting members occasionally to take to their corners.

*

You may not have realized it, but plans for the family vacation, as father has planned it, usually break down when he finally realizes that his wife has all day to lobby with the youngsters.

*

There is no place like home if the place is homelike.

*

A man's home can be his hassle.

*

Many a man has kept out of hot water by having a large family—and a small water heater.

*

After dinner, members of a lot of families suffer from dish-temper.

*

It isn't the pace of family life that throws you; it's the change of gears.

*

For many families, a recreation room is a necessity. After all, parents need someplace to go when their youngsters entertain.

*

FACT: Your home life will be happier if you kiss more, and cuss less.

*

Large families deserve a lot of credit—and they usually get it.

*

It's not strange that members of a family differ; even the lily family includes a cousin named garlic.

*

Any family of five or six kids is far happier than a family of five or six million dollars. The former doesn't keep straining for more.

*

Most families live from can to mouth.

*

Somehow home seemed jollier when it held a family with the housewife, the old man and the kids, instead of a spending unit with the homemaker, the senior citizen and the siblings.

*

The average family in the United States consists of 3.7 members. The .7 is the one who is laughingly referred to as the head of the house.

*

Money helps, but you can't make harmony in your home with only bank notes.

*

Things never run very smoothly in a home where the husband pulls out his watch in the kitchen.

*

Our private opinion is that you don't maintain a family circle by taking sides.

*

In most happy families, the pronouns "us" and "we" are used more frequently than "I."

*

Some statistician said recently that the average American family now has almost two cars as against a little more than one a few years back. All of which means that now mom has to lie awake until almost two cars get home.

*

History of a family: An apartment—a small house—a bigger house—a small house—and finally, back to an apartment.

*

FAMILY: A group of people whose trouble is that the youngsters grow out of childhood, but the parents never grow out of parenthood.

*

This you can believe: A family never has higher prestige than when it's described by a girl who is engaged to one of the sons.

*

Life is funny! Our family maintains a standard of living beyond its means because it is necessary to "keep up appearances." But when the neighbors do it, it's merely a case of "social climbing."

*

It is a little difficult at times to preserve peace in family jars.

*

The day of the old-fashioned large families seems to have passed. Maybe it's just as well, as the average breakfast nook couldn't accommodate them all.

*

The way we figure, it's the kind of heart, not the type of house, that makes a home.

*

A happy home is where both mates think they got better than they deserve.

*

The man who is loved by the house cat, the dog, the neighbor's children and his own wife and family is a great man, even though he never gets his name in *Who's Who*.

*

Some homes now have what they call a family room on the hopeful assumption that the family will stay home long enough to enjoy it.

*

These modern family rooms have put the living room in the same isolated status as Grandma's parlor.

*

Nowadays a family is a group of people who have keys to the same house.

*

Someone once said that some families are like a stable. The old man eats like a horse, the wife doesn't care a straw and chaffs at everybody all day, the son gives out with a lot of horse-radish, the daughter rides the high horse, and the whole family is saddled with a mortgage.

*

A close-knit family is one in which everybody makes socks and sweaters for everybody else.

*

Did you ever notice that when the mother of a large family goes out for an afternoon without taking one of the youngsters with her, she looks like the most relaxed person in the world—for an hour or so. Then the worry bug takes over.

*

Some families are like potatoes—the best part of them is underground.

*

A man doesn't really appreciate the meaning of family ties until his teen-age daughter becomes clothes conscious.

*

Modern psychologists demand that the whole family do things together, and yet when ma and the boys up in the hills helped pa shoot at the revenuers, they were criticized.

*

Maybe it would be well for every family to have a crisis now and then, if for no other reason than to keep the older folks reminded of how mature and responsible some of our teen-agers can be under pressure.

*

Happiness is one thing that multiplies by division.

*

Money doesn't necessarily make a man happy, but it sure keeps his creditors in a better frame of mind.

*

Some folks are as happy as they make up their minds to be—which could be about as happy as a traffic cop with flat feet.

*

Hunting for happiness is like hunting for lost sheep in the wilderness. If you ever find it the chances are that your only reward will be the locating of a mere skeleton.

*

Happy is the blonde who can keep her hair light and her past dark.

*

To be continually happy you've got to know when to be blind, when to be deaf and when to be dumb.

*

Happiness, like money, is not fully appreciated until it has disappeared.

*

Josh Billings once said: "The happiest man in the world is the one who has a good wife."

*

The happiest people are those who are too busy to notice.

*

The happiest man in the world is the one who knows what to remember in the past, what to enjoy in the present and what to plan in the future.

*

Some folks pursue happiness; others create it.

*

One reason some folks can never overtake happiness is that they pursue it trying to keep up with the Joneses.

*

Many a man's pursuit of happiness ends when his wife catches up with him.

*

The pursuit of happiness is guaranteed by the Constitution, but catching it is the tough job.

*

The pursuit of happiness is complicated by not knowing when you've found it.

*

In our pursuit of happiness we are greatly handicapped by having to take so many detours in an effort to dodge trouble.

*

Make somebody happy today. Mind your own business.

*

Most of the happiness in this world is found by folks who are not too doggone particular.

*

Some cause happiness wherever they go; others whenever they go.

*

To the modern wife, happiness is having a husband who likes to dine out.

*

To a boy, happiness could mean having a slingshot in a heaven full of greenhouses.

*

Money can't buy happiness, but there's sure a lot of us who are willing to make the experiment.

*

If you want to live happily ever after, don't be after too much.

*

Some fellows have a way of spreading happiness around. They wolf whistle at old maids.

*

Happiness is like jam. You can't spread even a little of it around without getting some on yourself.

*

Nothing upsets our own sense of values more than to meet a poor man who insists he is happy. We can't help wondering what his real angle is.

*

You never have to look for happiness if you're busy raising a nice family.

*

If there's ever a perfectly happy person to be found in this world, it will have to be one who has but little and doesn't care for too much.

*

Happy women talk; unhappy women write.

*

A lot of happiness is ruined because one of the hardest things to remember is to forget your petty troubles.

*

Happiness comes from living within your means. And that works pretty well on reducing too.

*

To be happy, take things as they come and let them go just as they came.

*

Be satisfied with a little. The atom has taken its split without beefing.

*

Money won't buy happiness, but it sure purchases the kind of misery some folks enjoy.

*

One way to keep happy is to learn to enjoy trouble.

*

Some folks aren't happy unless they have a bellyache.

*

It's pretty hard to tell what really does bring happiness; poverty and wealth have both failed.

*

The happiest man we can think of today is a vegetarian looking at the prices in the meat market.

*

Some folks seem to think the bluebird of happiness is just another swallow.

*

Someone once said that wishing for things brings more happiness than actually having them. Maybe so, but how about lower prices, reduced taxes and longing for lost youth?

*

There is plenty of happiness in this life if we only knew it, and one way to find out is this: When you have the old rheumatism, thank heaven it isn't the old gout.

*

Some folks claim they'd be happy if they had all the money they wanted. Others would be satisfied with less; they'd settle for just the money their creditors want.

*

You can't buy happiness with money, and you can't buy groceries with happiness—so it comes out about even.

*

Happiness is when a wife doesn't think she could do much better—and besides, she likes the guy.

*

There are times when the happiest man in the world is the fellow who is putting his mother-in-law on the train for home after a month's visit.

*

It takes just two things to make a girl happy these days. A roof over her head and a man under her thumb.

*

Happiness is like trouble—the more you nurse it, the bigger it gets.

*

TOAST: Here's to the happy days. Any darn fool can have a good time at night.

*

Some men find true happiness after marriage—providing their wives don't watch them too closely.

*

A woman isn't necessarily happy when she gets the man she wants, but she is when she gets the one man that every other girl wants.

*

Some folks are as naturally happy as a junkman looking through the modern woman's purse.

*

An old mammy's recipe for happiness was: "Don't let the seeds spoil your enjoyment of the watermelon; jest spit out the seeds."

*

Happiness is greater than money because folks enjoy it with you instead of figuring out a way to get it away from you.

*

Misery loves company, but happiness throws parties.

*

Some fellows never realize what happiness is until they get married; then it's too late.

*

A lot of times happiness will come through a door you didn't even know you left open.

*

If happiness could be bought, we'd probably be unhappy at the price tag.

*

A large number of people who are trying to find happiness have an extremely poor sense of direction.

*

To a lot of us happiness comes when we suddenly find ourselves in green fields, or "in the chips," so to speak.

*

A lot of happiness is overlooked because it doesn't cost anything.

*

It is a rare person who can simultaneously try to catch up with the Joneses and pursue happiness, because they are usually traveling in different directions.

*

Happiness, to a husband, is being called out of town on the day his mother-in-law is due to arrive.

*

Never miss an opportunity to make others happy, even if you have to leave them alone to do it.

*

When you learn to get along with everybody you quickly learn how scarce happiness isn't.

*

It was Jean Jacques Rousseau who said, "Happiness is made up of three things: a good bank account, a good cook and a good digestion."

*

Some men are never happy until something in a skirt comes along and makes them miserable.

*

Some folks are as naturally happy as a winning poker player reaching for a "pot" that has been built up after several hands.

*

Happiness is filling a kid's stomach, a woman's wardrobe and a man's billfold.

*

The more you work for it, the less you look for it, the quicker happiness comes.

*

Seems like a lot of us want life, liberty and happiness without too much pursuit.

*

Every man who thinks his neighbor is happier than he is should swap places with him. The result will be that he will want to swap back again in the morning.

*

Most of us fail to realize that whatever we do, or wherever we go, we take our happiness or unhappiness with us.

*

The foolish man seeks happiness in the distance; the wise man grows it under his own feet.

*

Most anyone can direct you to happiness. It's midway between too much and too little.

*

The secret of happiness is to learn to accept the impossible, do without the indispensable and bear the intolerable.

*

Always be happy. When the kettle is up to its neck in hot water, it still continues to sing.

*

White is a symbol of happiness. Could that be the reason a groom always wears black?

*

Searching for happiness is a good deal like hunting for wild berries. The best ones often are overlooked near at hand because of anticipating something better on the other side of the hill.

*

A poor man can be happy, but no happy man is ever poor.

*

By the way, just how happy would you be if you suddenly lost everything you had in the world, and then got it all back again?

*

Happiness is like potato salad. When you share it with others you have a picnic.

*

Never mistake pleasure for happiness. It's an entirely different breed of dog. There is a great deal of exquisite pleasure in happiness, but there is a great deal of pleasure that has no happiness in it.

*

One good way to find happiness is *not* by boring a hole to fit the plug, but by making a plug to fit the hole.

*

Dr. Albert Schweitzer once said: "Happiness is nothing more than good health and a bad memory."

*

You don't have to go out and look for happiness. Keep busy and it will find you without any trouble.

*

Happiness is that peculiar sensation you acquire when you are too busy to be miserable.

*

Folks are usually seeking more happiness when they are using only a small part of what they already have.

*

There is nothing we talk so fluently about as happiness—and nothing we know so little about.

*

The word "honeymoon," according to a professor of something or another, came from the custom of early American newlyweds to remain home for a month or so and feed honey to every caller. It was a sweet custom, no doubt. But times, in case you have forgotten, have changed. Today callers on newlyweds are usually just fed up.

*

HONEYMOON: The interval between the bridal toast and burnt toast.

*

After the honeymoon comes the tense transition from the past perfect to the future imperfect.

*

Many a good architect has discovered after the honeymoon that his wife can make plans too.

*

Many a honeymoon couple spend their first days in the sand and the rest of them on the rocks.

*

The bride's relatives, who during the honeymoon are in-laws, are afterward out-laws.

*

Newlyweds: If you want to fool the people in the hotel lobby when you're honeymooning, let the bride carry the luggage.

*

A CRAZY THING: A television set in a bridal suite.

*

The honeymoon is the thrill of a wifetime. It's the morning after the knot before.

*

HONEYMOON: A short period of doting between dating and debting.

*

After the honeymoon the girls usually stop wondering what to wear and start wondering how long it will.

*

Fellows: You promised her a "wine and candlelight honeymoon," so what's with this warm beer bit and that tired old flashlight?

*

A judge once said that a honeymoon is not a necessity. All we have to say is that the judge should pipe down. Uncle Sam might hear him and slap a luxury tax on honeymoons.

*

Modern-day honeymoons seem to be a brief period which two strangers who have recently married devote to getting acquainted with each other and wondering if they haven't been just a little too hasty after all. Especially when the groom takes his bride off the pedestal and puts her on a budget.

*

The honeymoon starts when the groom acts like a moon-struck calf, and ends when his wife becomes a little bossy.

*

"We have not yet begun to fight" was first said by a young couple on their honeymoon.

*

The most uncomfortable pair in the world is a honeymoon couple in an upper berth.

*

After the honeymoon, the first time a wife looks entirely satisfied with her husband is when his salary is raised.

*

HONEYMOON: The period of time during which the bride trusts the bridegroom's word of honor.

*

HOTEL SIGN: "Honeymooners treated with studied neglect."

*

Shoes are often thrown at the bride and groom, but they always furnish their own spats.

*

If you're planning a second honeymoon at Niagara Falls, you'd better not postpone it too long. Some experts believe that the falls, which are steadily receding, will be gone in another five thousand years.

*

The honeymoon is usually a vacation a man takes before going to work for a new boss.

*

The cooing usually stops when the honeymoon is over, but the billing goes on forever.

*

HONEYMOON: The short period between "I do!" and "You'd darn well better!"

*

Some fellows don't have too much fun on their honeymoon. They spend most of their time teaching their wife how to cook.

*

After the honeymoon an ideal often becomes an ordeal.

*

THE HONEYMOON IS OVER WHEN . . .

. . . she burns the dinner and he burns up.

*

. . . the fellow who won his bride with soft soap winds up washing the dishes.

*

. . . your prisoner of love becomes your ball and chain.

*

... she wants something around her neck besides his arms.

*

... her mother walks into the apartment with her own key.

*

... she quits crying on his shoulder and starts jumping down his neck.

*

... he starts wishing he'd married a good cooker instead of a good looker.

*

... he discovers the little lamb he married is just a wolf in she's clothing.

*

... they decide to convert the love seat into two TV chairs.

*

... he begins using bent paper clips for cuff links.

*

... he decides his bride is skinny instead of slender.

*

... he finds out he married a big spender—and she finds out she didn't.

*

... he stops whispering sweet nothings in her ear, and says nothing sweet.

*

... the groom quits asking, "Why, dear?" and simply sighs, "Well, OK."

*

... he finds out there are things he *can't* say with flowers.

*

... he stops helping with the dishes and does them himself.

*

... he discovers his wife was not made to order.

*

... her father begins to use his credit card.

*

... he no longer smiles gently as he scrapes the burnt toast.

*

... the baby talk is done by the baby.

*

... she stops lowering her eyes and starts raising her voice.

*

... what used to be your little "bug" becomes the fly in your ointment.

*

... the guy learns the bridal path can be a bit rough.

*

... he no longer blames the poor breakfast on the frying pan, the coffeepot or the toaster.

*

... he stops telling her she's as cute as a button, and begins telling her to button her lip.

*

... he begins to pay more attention to his financial shape than to her heavenly shape.

*

... she says, "I can't stand to drive with you—you make me nervous."

*

... he comes home to find his supper burning in the kitchen instead of the light burning in the window.

*

... she gets gabby, crabby and flabby.

*

... that sparkle in her eyes changes from a loving glow to a wicked gleam.

*

... he tells her they should name a hurricane after her.

*

... the groom learns that, instead of a keen-edged dart, Cupid hit him with a well-polished pan.

*

... her girl friends tell her she could have done a lot better.

*

... bushels of kisses are reduced to little pecks.

*

... the bride gets her first charge plate, and the groom gets the bills a month later.

*

... the ability to cook becomes important.

*

... they both cease to stifle their sighs and begin to stifle their yawns.

*

... he tells her that last year's dresses will do just fine this season.

*

... he doesn't notice that his wife is wearing something new until he gets the bill.

*

HUSBANDS

To be a good husband, a man has to be able to say in a dozen words what a woman says in a thousand.

*

The magician who saws a woman in half isn't nearly as marvelous as the husband who can keep her from flying to pieces.

*

The surest way for a husband to trip over something is to start running around too much.

*

HUSBANDS: Fellows who buy the frills, pay the bills and sign the wills.

*

Any husband who is right had better have an apology ready.

*

The puzzle most husbands can't solve is: The family has two cars, two bathrooms, two television sets, so how come they can't have two opinions around the house?

*

It doesn't do any good for a husband to put his foot down, because it will only be stepped on.

*

Many a breadwinner is treated like a crumb.

*

A lot of husbands have an impediment in their speech. Every time they open their mouth, the wife interrupts.

*

Husbands are men who are proud of their right to say what they please. The only trouble is, they wish they had the courage to do so.

*

HUSBANDS: Men who are captains of their soul—subject to their wives' control.

*

Lots of women admit that a husband is hard to find —and half the women admitting it are married.

*

When a fellow says he's on speaking terms with his wife, you can be sure she dictated the terms.

*

ADVICE TO WIVES: To keep a husband in good humor, just handle the old goat with kid gloves.

*

Most husbands know how to handle a wife, but their wives won't let them.

*

After a trip to the altar, some men never want to go anywhere else.

*

Many a husband gets an awful charge out of what his wife says.

*

Whenever a husband says he has things pretty much his own way at home, he usually means that his wife takes command of the youngsters, the money, the cat, the dog and the canary—and he can say what he pleases about the goldfish.

*

*The handy man who makes life sunny
Is a husband handy with the money.*

*

Most husbands, just in case you give a darn, girls, love the kind of wife who wears everything well—except the pants.

*

Nowadays one of the most costly things a husband has to face is keeping up his wife's.

*

Traffic experts claim that husbands are much better drivers than bachelors. Well, why shouldn't they be? Look at all the help they get.

*

WELL-INFORMED HUSBAND: One whose wife has just told him what she thinks of him.

*

Whenever a wife lets the husband do the talking, that husband isn't hers.

*

Some fellows are a failure as husbands because they can never remember which dish towel is for show only.

*

By the time a man has learned to handle his wife, the kids are doing it.

*

When the average husband looks around and sees the kind of men most women marry, he can't help thinking that his wife has done mighty well for herself.

*

Nothing reminds a woman of something that needs to be done around the house like a husband who is taking it easy.

*

The guilty look on her husband's face is usually the key that unlocks a wife's intuition.

*

HUSBAND: A gay blade who had one close shave too many.

*

Husbands are easy to handle. All a girl has to do is to keep on crying.

*

Most husbands go about their household repair projects in fits and starts—they have a fit every time they have to start one.

*

If husbands really want to stay out of the doghouse, they should never pick a bone.

*

Husbands who are allowed one night a week at their club are like an old horse turned into pasture. They want to cut up a bit but have forgotten how.

*

A modern husband is a do-it-yourself man with a get-it-done wife.

*

HUSBAND: A guy who is king in his own home if he has plenty of jack and leaves the queen alone. Otherwise the silly ace will get the deuce.

*

Any husband can usually help his wife make up her mind by simply voicing his opinion.

*

Almost any husband can keep his wife guessing. The only trouble is, she usually guesses right.

*

There's just too darn much expected of husbands by our modern-day brides. They believe that when he brings home the bacon, he ought to fry it too.

*

Husbands are usually very responsible men. In fact, most wives claim they are responsible for all their troubles.

*

ADVICE TO WIVES: Some husbands are like an egg. If you keep him in hot water long enough, he'll get hard-boiled.

*

Many a husband looks run-down, because of the bills his wife runs up.

*

The average husband doesn't know his failings, but his wife keeps a long list of them.

*

There are two things that will test a husband's love for his wife. Her cold feet and her hot temper!

*

A confiding husband is one who promptly tells his wife anything he feels she is bound to find out anyway.

*

It's a smart husband who thinks twice before he says nothing.

*

Husbands are what most women have always wanted —a combination of father, lover, husband, child, enemy, back scratcher and foot warmer.

*

Why is it that every time a husband comes home with his mind made up to stay home, his wife has her face made up to go out?

*

Good husbands, to some wives, are those who put up when asked, and shut up when told.

*

Some husbands claim they lead a dog's life, and maybe they do. They come in with muddy feet, make themselves comfortable in an easy chair and wait to be fed.

*

It's all right for a husband to be a breadwinner, but how come so many wives expect him to be a bakery?

*

If men continue to tie aprons around their waists, it won't be long before we'll be hearing women say: "I don't want to hurt your feelings, honey, but you're not the cook my father was."

*

Ever notice how much more abuse a woman can take from a poor husband than she can from a rich one?

*

You may hear a man brag now and then that he wears the pants in the family, but you can lay a heavy bet that it's his wife who selects them.

*

A European psychiatrist once said that if the typical American husband weren't so darned weak-kneed, he'd assert his right to be the head of the home in actuality. Well, I guess maybe the typical American husband prefers weak knees to broken legs.

*

To learn about women, ask the man who is owned by one.

*

The husband who promised to move heaven and earth for his bride is the same fellow who, a few years later, growls all over the place when he's asked to move the sofa.

*

HUSBAND: A bachelor who solicited directions.

*

There are two kinds of husband. One brings his wife a gift when returning from a convention or other out-of-town trip; the other behaved himself.

*

*A man can go through married life without an angry word
    or fight,
If he'll just shut up when he's wrong and keep still when
    he's right.*

*

There is no husband on earth who is more appreciated than the one who agrees with his wife that she is wonderful.

*

There are two sides to most husbands: The side their wives know, and the side they think their wives don't know.

*

The only time a typical husband makes a decision is when he buzzes for an elevator.

*

There are some men who would never make a good husband. They just can't seem to get along with women—their disposition is too peaceful.

*

Would you believe there's buried treasure in this country? If you don't think so, just listen to some women talk about their first husband.

*

A husband is less likely to be neglected if he is suspected.

*

There are lots of things a husband would like to forget—but his wife won't let him.

*

The reason why married men are often tied down is that more wives than husbands know the ropes.

*

When an old bachelor talks to himself,
It's a sign of approaching senility—
But when a long-married man talks to himself,
It's a sign of marital hostility.

*

Few husbands these days get bombarded by cups and saucers—but most all of them are hit hard now and then by charge plates.

*

Husbands who refuse to stand for their wives' extravagance may take it sitting down.

*

Women prefer husbands with a will of their own—providing it's made out in her name.

*

All the majority of husbands want from their wives is affection, encouragement and the ability to live grand and comfortable on an inadequate income.

*

A husband is a guy who knows very little about women's clothes—except that they keep him broke.

*

One of a husband's toughest problems is getting back some of the take-home pay he has so dutifully taken home.

*

A husband can make his wife do almost anything—if he's a hypnotist.

*

A wise husband never contradicts his wife. He just waits around for a while and she will contradict herself.

*

Some men are husbands merely because some woman disliked being called an old maid.

*

Some husbands are real comforters, while others are just wet blankets.

*

There are times in the life of every husband when he's sure he was meant to be a bachelor.

*

An archaeologist is the best husband any woman can have. The older she gets, the more interested he is in her.

*

Domestic harmony is music produced only if the husband plays second fiddle.

*

War veterans are fellows who wear ribbons on their chests, while veteran husbands are those who have to be content with lines on their brows.

*

If a wife goes home to her mother, her husband is a brute—but if a husband goes home to his mother, he's just a plain coward.

*

A husband may be an accountant but still be unable to figure his wife out.

*

Whenever a husband seems happy and contented, his wife makes up her mind that one of these days she's going to find out why.

*

A perfect husband sets a bad example for the rest of the married men.

*

Few husbands carry an up-to-date photo of their wife after she hits forty.

*

Husbands are former bachelors whose luck finally failed.

*

Views expressed by husbands are not necessarily those of the management.

*

Being a husband is like any other job. It helps a lot if you like the boss.

*

Whenever a man admits that he sees eye-to-eye with his wife, you can take it for granted that his vision has been corrected.

*

For every man who speaks from experience, there are a dozen who don't get a chance to.

*

ADVICE TO HUSBANDS: Never trust your wife's judgment! Look who she married!

*

Some husbands may not be so hot at bringing home the bacon, but they're usually experts at spilling the beans.

*

When a husband stops bringing home the bacon, his goose is cooked.

*

There are some girls who can't take a joke, while others prefer one to no husband at all.

*

One shining example of married life is the pair of trousers many a husband has to wear.

*

To some women, the perfect husband is one whom she can yell at without fear of being answered back.

*

PACIFICATION PROGRAM: A husband bringing his wife flowers after an argument.

*

Women love their sons and fathers—but their husbands they just put up with.

*

The average husband never worries too much about who is the boss in the family—but where she is.

*

Among the uglier things behind the headlines these days are husbands who don't shave before breakfast.

*

HUSBAND: A fellow who believes that his wife's constant chattering is just one of life's little *ear*itations.

*

The way we figure, a husband is a lot like a shapely movie actress trying to duck photographers—he never knows just when he's going to be snapped at.

*

Some men are under the impression that they boss the house, but the truth is that they only house the boss.

*

A lot of the boys who claim they are not the least bit superstitious will, somehow or another, pay attention to signs when the little woman makes them.

*

A noted astronomer once said that when a comet nears "home" after a prolonged absence, it develops a most unbelievable tail. Well, we might add that so do some husbands, if you change the spelling slightly.

*

HUSBAND: A fellow for whom the bills toll.

*

Why is it that when a husband smiles, his wife always wants to know why?

*

NOTE TO HUSBANDS: Honey is both soothing and healing. The man who has whispered it to his wife can understand this.

*

Don't be so sure that you can always identify a married man when you see one—it just might be a bachelor with a grouch.

*

DEFIANT HUSBAND: One who slams the door of the doghouse.

*

Some husbands are like unsuccessful playwrights—they never have a show.

*

It's no use for a husband to put his foot down when he hasn't a leg to stand on.

*

HUSBAND: An unfortunate who began by handing out a line and ended up by toeing it.

*

The man who doesn't tell his wife everything probably figures that what *she* doesn't know won't hurt *him*.

*

Inflation is a state of affairs when you never had it so good—or parted with it so fast.

*

In the desert they have mirages. Inflation is a similar illusion, except that it's money, not water, that really isn't there.

*

By the time a family acquires a nest egg these days, inflation has turned it into chicken feed.

*

Passing the buck is not new, but bucks never passed faster than they do these days.

*

Inflation has one good point. Your kids can't get sick on a nickel's worth of candy.

*

Unless we all begin to holler
We soon may have a five-cent dollar.

*

A little inflation is like a little pregnancy—it keeps on growing.

*

Some of our Congressmen say they think the buying power of the dollar should be stabilized. Personally, we think it should be resurrected.

*

Nowadays, with all this inflation, if you give a bum a nickel he hands it back with another nickel. He thinks you're the bum.

*

I suspect the only way to head off inflation is to bring dollars and sense back together.

*

INFLATION: An ill wind that does everybody—but good!

*

With all the money floating around, inflation would be a wonderful thing—if it weren't for the high prices.

*

Seems like inflation is a method of cutting a dollar bill in half without damaging the paper.

*

Believe it or not, but this inflation business is like a whirlwind where you have to run twice as fast merely to stay in the same place.

*

INFLATION: When the dollar doesn't go as far as it once did, but the acceleration is much better developed.

*

The average penny-pincher now brings up his son to be a nickel-squeezer.

*

Thanks to inflation, you can live it up these days without going off your diet.

*

Inflation is the only thing that people are down on that's on the up and up.

*

Money gets around so fast these days that the term "jumping jack" has taken on a new meaning.

*

Inflation is here when money that once talked turkey hardly says beans.

*

An economist once said that inflation is mostly psychological. Well, maybe so, but all we know is that this psychological situation is keeping us slightly broke.

*

Some "experts" look upon inflation as a sensible economic operation. Cripes! We'll bet these same guys would fall into fits of uncontrollable laughter at the sight of a dog chasing its own tail.

*

Inflation is when you earn four or five dollars an hour and, in the supermarket, your wife spends at the rate of six dollars a minute.

*

At least inflation isn't dull. It's truly fascinating to see how much money you can go broke on these days.

*

Inflation continues to devaluate money, and you may console yourself with the thought that the dollar you haven't got isn't worth much anyway.

*

Having trouble making ends meet? Maybe it's because inflation has stretched them too far apart.

*

Today, with all this inflation going on, about all you can get for a dollar is a picture of George Washington.

*

FACT: Folding money is now collapsing currency.

*

The way we figure, inflation is when those who have saved for a rainy day really get soaked.

*

Stop inflation! The business you save may be your own.

*

During these days of inflation and cheap money, when anyone says they feel like a million dollars, they are, in fact, about half sick. That may not be economics-textbook language, but it amounts to this, to make the point perfectly clear: The guy has a sinking feeling.

*

Give inflation a little more time
And wooden nickels will cost a dime.

*

Inflation is a condition where, instead of not having the money you don't have, you have twice as much but it's worth only half of what you don't have now.

*

INFLATION: When you can't get something for nothing, but you can get next to nothing for something.

*

According to our politicians, inflation is a terrible thing that happens to the normal upward adjustment of prices whenever the opposition is in power.

*

Inflation is when the crashing pillars of the economic system can't be heard above the rustling banknotes.

*

After the trip to the top of the inflation spiral has been made, the return trip will be made by another and much speedier means—the toboggan slide.

*

Inflation is when a man can lose his shirt not only in the stock market but in the supermarket as well.

*

With this inflation business, vegetarians are not the only ones who don't eat meat.

*

A coin's life is said to be about twenty-five years, but just take a look at what inflation does to its value in that time.

*

This you can believe: Inflation is agreeable only to the manufacturers of falsies—but only to their kind of inflation.

*

FACT: Production is the answer to inflation. That's why rabbit fur is cheaper than mink.

*

Today, if you should be lucky enough to make a good "pile," you have to hire an accountant to explain how you did it.

*

INFLATION: A national headache caused by asset indigestion.

*

In these days of spiraling inflation, the person with a fixed income is really in a fix.

*

The march of inflation plays curious tricks. What used to cost about ten dollars to buy now costs twenty to fix.

*

What with inflation, strikes and tie-ups these days, about the only bird who can guarantee delivery of anything is the stork.

*

Confidentially, the most dangerous type of inflation is a swelled head.

*

It's gotten so that small boys begging money from strangers refuse to bite anything less than a fifty-cent piece.

*

The way we figure, inflation is being broke with a pocketful of money.

*

Everything is going up—and that includes women's skirts.

*

The trouble with trying to build a nest egg these days is that inflation is likely to shrink it from extra-large to sparrow-size by the time you have need of it.

*

INFLATION: That means your money won't buy as much today as it would during the depression, when you didn't have any.

*

Everybody is against inflation in general, but anxious for a little of it personally.

*

In these times of inflation our dollar is drawn and quartered.

*

Inflation is when the difference between what you make and what you spend is what you owe.

*

What this country really needs is a Sanforized dollar bill—shrinkproof.

*

There are those who claim we don't have too much inflation in this great and wondrous nation. Yeah? Well, if that's so, how come a hot dog that I used to buy complete with mustard and pickle now costs a nickel for the pickle?

*

In these days of inflation it's virtually an insult to tell a girl she looks like a million dollars.

*

INFLATION: A drop in the buck.

*

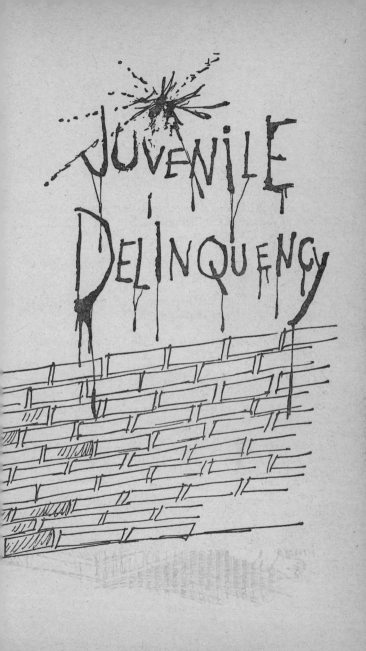

Delinquency wasn't one of the crosses
When dad and mom were the bosses.

*

I suspect the reason we have so many juvenile delinquents in America today is because their dads didn't burn their britches behind them.

*

There are times when you can straighten out a youngster by bending him over.

*

Juvenile delinquency is the result of parents trying to raise their kids without starting at the bottom.

*

A delinquency cure is a rawhide applied to the kid's backside.

*

Littering the streets is bad, of course. But there wasn't so much juvenile delinquency in the days when a boy could easily find an old tin can to kick along the way to and from school.

*

Wonder if juvenile delinquency started about the time that men quit wearing top hats for little boys to throw snowballs at?

*

Some folks grow up and still remain juvenile and delinquent.

*

Most juvenile delinquents are home-grown.

*

EGGS: What kids grow up to be when their parents are chicken.

*

144

There are a lot of senile delinquents too, and they'd be worse than juvenile delinquents if they only had the strength.

*

A psychiatrist once said: "A considerable percentage of juvenile delinquency is due to a defect in the parent's own integration in certain areas of behavior." Translation: Many problem children result from bad examples set by parents.

*

JUVENILE DELINQUENT: A kid who prefers vice to advice.

*

Many of our minors are becoming major problems.

*

Parents are always being blamed for juvenile delinquency, but I don't know. Chickens come from broken homes and *they* turn out all right.

*

One rotten egg doesn't spoil a dozen—but it sure does when they're scrambled.

*

Maybe one reason for so much juvenile delinquency is that we provide youngsters with more critics than examples.

*

When the electric age put the old-time woodshed out of business, that was the time we began hearing so much about juvenile delinquency. Too many woodsheds have been converted into garages. In fact, they didn't call it juvenile delinquency in the old days, because father had a woodshed and a razor strap to combat it.

*

There was a time when, if a kid started sowing wild oats, his dad started the thrashing machine.

*

The prevalence of juvenile delinquency is proving that parents are not getting at the seat of the problem.

*

There were fewer delinquents in the old days, and most of them found sitting down very painful.

*

Juvenile delinquency is the modern term for what we did when we were kids.

*

The trouble with some of today's smart kids is that they don't smart in the right place.

*

Maybe the reason we have so much juvenile delinquency is that the parents have so many meetings with the teachers, nobody's home watching the kids.

*

We understand authorities are making plans for forestry camps to combat juvenile delinquency. This may be a good idea, but how long can we grown-ups hide out there?

*

We don't have to worry about Russia coming over here. Let's face it, we've got the best armed juvenile delinquents in the world.

*

Teen-age delinquents are kids who wildly roam
Because they have no parental restraint at home.

*

A juvenile delinquent is the result of the sins of the fathers being visited upon the children to the point where the sins of the children are visited upon the city fathers.

*

Remember the old days, when a juvenile delinquent was a kid who owed a few cents on an overdue book at the library?

*

The way we figure, maybe the thing that's wrong with this generation is that too many slippers are being worn out on the dancing floors.

*

JUVENILE DELINQUENT: A youngster who has plenty of will power, but even more won't power.

*

The best time to tackle a minor problem is before he gets big enough to strike back.

*

Some delinquents have been arrested for cutting off a girl's hair. Just goes to show you what some of these "snips" will do.

*

Maybe the reason so many youngsters are seen on the streets at night is that they're afraid to stay home—alone!

*

JUVENILE DELINQUENT: A boy who begins acting like his father.

*

There wasn't so much talk about juvenile delinquency back in the days when the family Bible held a prominent spot in the home, or when studies were taught "to the tune of the hickory stick." Today, some of the kids seem to think the three *R*'s are Rock, Roll and Rebel.

*

Wonder if it would help to fight juvenile delinquency by getting the kids interested in bowling? At least it would get them off the streets—and into the alleys!

*

Another way to reduce juvenile delinquency sharply would be to quit coddling hard-boiled eggs.

*

Maybe juvenile delinquency could be cured if more parents would start rapping their bundles from heaven.

*

Our personal opinion is that the juvenile problem is not so much of ruling the youngsters with a firm hand as it is of using a firm hand with a ruler.

*

A wise old sage once remarked that the action of some children suggests that their parents embarked on the Sea of Matrimony without a paddle. What he might have meant is: What this country needs is a lot more old-fashioned woodsheds, and less child-psychology books written by old bachelors.

*

In the old days when a woodshed stood behind every American home, a great deal of what now passes for juvenile delinquency was settled out of court. That just goes to prove that a lot of this juvenile delinquency business is due to parents being asleep at the switch.

*

There was a time in the old days when, if Junior showed symptoms of delinquency, the treatment was prompt and efficient. He was taken to pop's psychiatric clinic in the woodshed for razor-strap therapy. This was usually followed by around fourteen hours of confinement in bed without benefit of nourishment.

*

Our private opinion is that the safety razor is responsible for juvenile delinquency. It put the razor strap out of business.

*

Cheer up! Last year some twenty million boys and girls between the ages of ten and seventeen were *not* picked up by the police for any crime whatsoever.

*

Juvenile delinquent: A kid who sows his wild oats while his parents pray for a crop failure.

*

One reason for juvenile delinquency is that many parents are raising their youngsters by remote control.

*

Fact: The increasingly large number of juvenile delinquents shows that appeasement also fails to work in the rearing of children.

*

Whether the kid you have in mind is a hopeless delinquent or merely a high-spirited youngster "passing through a phase" depends on whether he happens to be the youngster in the next block or your own kid.

*

In the old days the "bad boys," as they were called, stole apples and watermelons. Today it's hub caps and gasoline.

*

Let's not panic in the matter of juvenile delinquency. After all, a lot of kids go around unarmed until they're twelve or fourteen years of age.

*

Love is not a thing to be taken lightly. Maybe that's why lovers like to turn out the light.

*

When you come right down to plain, simple facts, more men have been caught with lipstick than with finger-prints.

*

Sometimes it's safer to carry a torch than try to put out the flame.

*

Love is a four-letter word that often spells trouble.

*

The significance of a long courtship is that the girl has looked and looked, and finally realized she can do no better.

*

The apple of a man's eye often turns out to be forbidden fruit.

*

Many a guy who hands a girl a line finds himself tied with it.

*

Someone once said that Cupid is a life saver, but that's ridiculous! He pushes you right into the Sea of Matrimony.

*

The fellow who turns a girl's head often ends up being a pain in the neck.

*

The way we figure, any guy will go to bat for a girl with good curves.

*

Many a girl has found a knotty problem at the end of a smooth line.

*

Fellows: If you're shedding tears over an old petti-coat, dry them with a new skirt.

*

Every girl has a mental picture of the man she wants to marry, and if she doesn't get the one she wants, heaven help the one she gets.

*

Love at first sight may be all right, but it depends a lot on who's in sight.

*

To a love-sick guy, his pretty girl is like a malady.

*

Dark corners are where fellows get bright ideas.

*

Many a guy gets into deep water trying to make a splash.

*

Sometimes when a fellow gives a girl a big hand, she never knows what he has up his sleeve.

*

If a fellow looks a girl right in the eye, he may be missing other things she hoped he'd notice.

*

Just because a girl prefers a man with "lettuce" doesn't mean she's a vegetarian.

*

It may be love that makes the world go round, but it's marriage that keeps most of the inhabitants hustling.

*

Love is like seasickness. However, there is this differ-ence. For seasickness you take a pill; in love you marry him.

*

Girls who keep angling are often left dangling.

*

Fellows: Don't keep telling her you are unworthy of her; she knows it!

*

If love is blind, why are so many men attracted to a beautiful woman?

*

FACT: Many a young man has browsed through his girl friend's family album, but failed to heed its warning.

*

Do you realize what happens to nine out of ten men who fall in love? They get married!

*

WARNING: It's a lot easier, fellows, to live with two hundred pounds of curves than one hundred pounds of nerves.

*

Let's face it, a good pair of legs can get a person to first base—even if she isn't a baseball player.

*

Many a man has lost his shirt while pressing his suit.

*

Many times a girl thinks it's the real thing, but it turns out to be only a passing fiancé.

*

When the right girl comes along she will bring out the wolf in mother's little lamb.

*

When a girl's heart beats like a drum, it's usually a call to arms.

*

A girl who doesn't have the curves usually plays all the angles.

*

Any girl who sets a man a-quiver with admiration usually finds it easy to shake him down.

*

A lot of girls have been carried away on the wings of love but have had to find their way back on their own shoe leather.

*

When a woman is in love she goes into ecstasy, while the fellow goes to the bank.

*

When you walk into a park you know that love is a great game. In fact, it's the only game I can think of off-hand where the players are content to stay on the bench.

*

In the garden of love a lot of girls are just a spring bud, but as soon as they find the right bud they'll spring!

*

Fellows: She may use the best brand of eyewash, but she can still give you a dirty look.

*

This you can believe: Many a man's goose has been cooked by getting a girl all steamed up.

*

When it comes to making love, some men figure they are the man of the hour—and the girl has to watch every minute.

*

Most lovers have their big moments in the small hours.

*

Love can cause high blood pressure or a stomachache, so the doctors tell us. Maybe that's the reason some young couples look so sick.

*

From our observation, it seems the aim of every girl is to get a ring job before her model becomes obsolete.

*

Sometimes love is like taking pictures—you're never sure how it will turn out.

*

Liquor and love have a lot in common. After six years they're both old stuff.

*

Whenever a man has a bee in his bonnet, he usually has a honey on his mind.

*

When a girl says she'll play ball with a fellow, you can take it for granted she plans to be the catcher.

*

The man who fiddles around rarely gets to lead the orchestra.

*

A French doctor once said that being in love offers the best immunity to colds. Just to be doubly sure, though, it might be well to have a couple of aspirins handy.

*

The girl who sighs, "Will you love me when I'm old and gray?" should stop asking such silly questions and make the most of her time while she's young.

*

Love is blind, so they tell us, and I suspect there are a lot of fellows who, when they bring out a picture of an old flame, are convinced that they must have been cock-eyed.

*

Lots of girls fall in love with a convertible that isn't paid for.

*

It's usually a fellow's "dream boat" that keeps him awake.

*

A lot of fellows fall in love with a girl who has soft brown eyes, warm red lips—and cool long green.

*

To a girl who has been in love only once, it's always a serious matter, but after six or seven times, she pays about as much attention to it as she does a stop sign.

*

Love may laugh at locksmiths, but landlords and supermarkets sure make it wipe that silly grin off its face.

*

SMART GIRL: One who can tell the difference between being bitten by a love bug and a louse.

*

The way we figure, if a girl expects to win a husband she ought to exhibit her generous nature—or else how generous nature has been to her.

*

Many a love nest has been broken up by a lark.

*

Life without a spark of love has caused many a girl to start playing with fire.

*

TOAST: Here's to love—that which begins with a fever and ends with a yawn.

*

Lovers satisfy their appetites on the mysteries of their delirium, but after they are married and the pork and beans are brought in, they have a fair chance to test the real qualities of their appetites.

*

In the beginning it was the apple that caused Adam to slip, but these days it's more apt to be a peach.

*

Most men acquire a polish after a girl has taken a shine to them.

*

There's many a beau ends up by playing second fiddle.

*

Horsing around too much has caused many a man to wind up as a groom.

*

GIRLS: The guy to be suspicious of is the one who pops in when pop's out.

*

Love is a friendship that gets all loused up.

*

Some folks claim that love is peace, quiet and rest, but that's ridiculous! That's not love! That's sleep.

*

When she begins knitting a guy a sweater, it's time for him to begin knitting his brow.

*

The greatest drawback to a budding love affair is the blooming expense.

*

I've noticed that the first thing a spark of love does is burn a hole in a fellow's pocket.

*

A girl can lose a good catch by letting out too much line.

*

The guy who is head over heels in love will soon be up to his neck in debt.

*

Love may make your heart beat faster and your skin get flushed, but ask your old grandpappy about that. A flight of stairs does the same thing for him.

*

There's only one cure for a man in love, and that's a good dose of marriage. If that doesn't cure him, nothing will.

*

Quite often love comes to a girl in the flash of a bankroll.

*

Love is a beautiful story—and marriage is the talking version of the same play.

*

Many a dull girl shines in the dark.

*

When you're necking in the parlor and you hear a noise upstairs—it's a good idea to listen, look and stop!

*

It's been said that love is the key to happiness, but you've got to be sure to pick the right lock.

*

Two is company—and three is the result.

*

Our private opinion is that these days the girls don't marry a man to reform him. They want to get in on the fun themselves.

*

Most lessons in love are learned in night school.

*

FACT: Even Cupid crosses his fingers at some of the things he hears by moonlight.

*

You know that civilization doesn't always time things right. For instance, in the old days lipstick could have been wiped off those old celluloid collars.

*

Fellows: If you want to know how she'll talk to you after you marry her, just listen to the way she talks to her little brother.

*

If you're bent on marrying the girl, old buddy, go ahead! She'll soon straighten you out.

*

As soon as a girl has a guy going around in circles, she knows he'll soon be dizzy enough to marry her.

*

Most girls are looking for a man who is tall, dark and has some.

*

Ever notice how Cupid loves to play with matches?

*

Love is like a vaccination: When it takes, you don't have to be told.

*

Any time a girl starts putting on the dog, she's through with puppy love.

*

The term "falling in love" is used because this doesn't happen to people until they lose their balance.

*

It's hard for a girl to keep cool when the right man warms her up.

*

The oldest plastic material in the world is a love-stricken boy in the hands of a girl.

*

Sometimes love starts beside a babbling brook—and ends up over a leaky kitchen sink.

*

Many a heaving bosom is nothing but a hope chest.

*

Love may be blind, but a diamond sparkler is a sure eye-opener.

*

A new flame may be hot stuff, but the old one knows what's cooking.

*

Love, according to the lyric writers of popular songs, is a sad and rocky road.

*

The progress a fellow makes with a girl depends a lot on the oil he uses—crude or refined.

*

A little soft soap can make a man slip.

*

Love cuts up all sorts of monkey shines. It makes a fool sober and a wise man frisky.

*

Love doesn't really make the world go round. It just makes people dizzy.

*

In love, a woman's heart is steel, a man's heart is flint. When the two of them come together that makes a match, and a lot of guy's find out real soon which end the sulphur is on.

*

Many a girl who fits into a man's arms doesn't fit into his pocketbook.

*

Give a man enough rope and he'll get himself all tangled up with some woman.

*

Love is that magic ingredient that turns bread to cake, weeds to roses and bachelors to idiots.

*

When a backward girl falls in love she has something to look forward to.

*

Sometimes when a girl finds the man she wants to marry for love, she discovers he has no money.

*

The one way a girl can stop a man from making love to her is to marry him.

*

When a girl begins hammering away at a man, the chances are she's planning on nailing him.

*

Love has been called a lot of things, but it'll always remain just one silly thing after another.

*

Love is when you woo a wow without a whoa.

*

When a girl in love makes a play for a diamond, that proves that she isn't stone blind.

*

Many a young lover has to start from scratch because he got a little rash.

*

Often, taking a girl in his arms leads to a fellow having her on his hands.

*

The girl who uses her head usually has a shoulder to put it on.

*

Soft shoulders cause accidents in more ways than one.

*

Girls: Just because a man is polished is no sign he has a clean mind.

*

The course of true love never runs up a big light bill.

*

Fellows: Never run after women! You can stroll along leisurely and get mixed up with more of them than you'll ever know what to do with.

*

The trouble with a lot of girls is that they can't decide whether they want a man who is old and bent, or one who is young and broke.

*

When a girl gets hungry for love it means she's fed up with being single.

*

Any girl can handle the beast in a man—if she's cagey enough.

*

MARRIAGE

If marriages are made in heaven, how come so many couples fight like the devil?

*

When a fellow is single he often lies awake thinking of something she said. After marriage, he won't fall asleep until after she's finished saying it.

*

Marriage is a lot like a game of cards. It starts off with a pair. He shows a diamond. She shows a flush. There's a big shuffle and they wind up with a full house.

*

All men are born free and equal! If they get married, that's their fault.

*

On the Sea of Matrimony, many a dream boat becomes a battleship.

*

A man can never really appreciate how a performer feels when he plays to an empty house until he tries to tell his wife a funny story.

*

Marriage is a man's course in domestic silence.

*

Before marriage the girl may say, "I just *love* to see a man smoking a pipe!" After marriage the tune is often changed to: "I'd just like to see you *try* to smoke that smelly old pipe in this house!"

*

Despite talks for world peace, marriage statistics continue to show an increase.

*

If a married couple don't like the same thing, *he*'s out of luck.

*

Keep your eyes open before marriage; after that it doesn't matter so much—you're not going anywhere.

*

After a man has been married for a year or so it slowly dawns on him that he is only the assistant head of the house.

*

The practice of putting women on pedestals began to die out when men found out that the girls could give orders better from that position.

*

Marriage resembles a detective story. It's full of surprises and you never know just how it's going to turn out.

*

If you marry on a shoestring, you're in for a good lacing.

*

You can always tell when a marriage is shaky. The partners don't even talk to each other during a television commercial.

*

The only thing some couples have in common is that they were married in the same church.

*

Some folks say marriage is a joke. Try it sometime and see how many laughs you get out of it.

*

Some couples are like a pair of lovebirds. They're always flying at each other.

*

A man never knows about the opposite sex until he gets married—then he finds out just how opposite they are.

*

The *witch*ing hour in marriage is when the wife meets the old man at the door with that awful question "*Which* story is it this time?"

*

In marriage it's foolish for a man to worry about anything beyond his control—such as his wife.

*

To most married men, a stitch in time is a complete surprise.

*

Most wives have a terrible memory—they never forget anything.

*

Two things a lot of married men will never forget: Pearl Harbor and their wedding day—they were both sneak attacks.

*

When some girls think of marriage they have hopes of their ship coming in, but usually all they get is a raft of kids.

*

It's been said that very few women have much knowledge of parliamentary law, but that's ridiculous! Ask any married man who's the speaker of the house.

*

A marriage really settles down after he and she have checked and learned there is no rich relative likely to leave anything to anyone.

*

After marriage some girls stop dropping their eyes and start raising their voices.

*

Some marriages are an open-and-shut affair. He opens his mouth and she shuts it.

*

Marriage is a fifty-fifty proposition in a lot of homes. He tells her what to do, and she tells him where to go.

*

Some fellows have gotten married on a bet, and spent the rest of their lives crusading against gambling.

*

After being swept off their feet into marriage, it's surprising how many girls lose interest in a broom.

*

Not every man who sleeps with a battle-ax is an Indian.

*

The man who marries for looks usually spends the rest of his life getting dirty ones.

*

Some women marry a man because he's a gay dog, and then spend all their time hounding him about it.

*

Some couples who get married just for a lark really do get the bird.

*

A girl will marry for money, but most men marry for a fancy figure.

*

Only girls get married; fellows get "took."

*

It's dangerous for a man to marry a woman who looks good in black.

*

Most men marry for looks—but not the kind they get when they come home late for dinner.

*

There's something to be said for marriage, but who has the nerve?

*

Marriage is called the Sea of Matrimony because it's so hard to keep your head above water.

*

Every husband knows what happens when his wife's temper gets away from her. He catches it.

*

It really doesn't matter if a fellow is man or mouse. In the end some cat usually gets him anyway.

*

Nothing makes a man quit spending money on a girl like a good dose of marriage.

*

The girl who married a man to mend his ways is likely to learn he isn't worth a darn.

*

Remember your song when you first fell in love? And you've been dancing to her music ever since, haven't you?

*

There is no such thing as marriage ties. The wife always wins.

*

From the moment a man says, "I do!" it'll most likely be his wife who decides whether he does or not.

*

Before marriage a girl embraces a man, but after marriage she puts the squeeze on him.

*

You never know when you're going to get hooked in marriage. Many a man has taken his girl through the tunnel of love, only to learn later that she was carrying an anchor.

*

Some fellows have been married for as long as twenty-five years and their wives are still appealing to them—to stop gambling, to stop drinking and to stop smoking.

*

A lot of wives are too bright to be kept in the dark about some old flame.

*

One reason for unhappy marriages is that men can't fool their wives as they did their mothers.

*

Marriage seems to sober up a lot of couples after they've been intoxicated with love for a spell.

*

Marriage is like a midnight phone call: You get a ring and then you wake up.

*

Few things contribute more to a happy married life than having all the wife's suitors turn out to be even worse bums than the one she married.

*

Many a young girl whose dream of marriage was highly colored has found it was only a pigment of her imagination.

*

Marriage is when a fellow gives a girl plenty of rope and wakes up to find himself tied in a knot.

*

When there's a meeting of minds in marriage, the wife usually presides.

*

Many a man has been stung trying to get a little honey for himself.

*

Girls who are described as a ball of fire are always looking for a guy with money to burn.

*

Marriage makes it easy for a man to find out what charming men his wife used to go out with.

*

Marriage

There are couples who have been married so long they've actually reached the point where they have mutual feelings. They hate each other.

*

When a girl's figure is shipshape there are a lot of guys who want to be her first mate.

*

Often a soft-spoken girl changes into an oft-spoken wife, and the guy has about as much chance of getting a word in edgewise as a woodpecker has of making a hole in a concrete telephone pole.

*

They keep telling us that marriage is a fifty-fifty proposition, but did you ever hear of a wife sharing her clothes closet with her husband?

*

Some couples have a real "football romance." They sit around every day waiting for the other to kick off.

*

When a man proposes to a gal and tells her that if she will marry him she will never want for anything, that shows how little he knows about women.

*

One of the first things a man finds out after he gets married is that intelligence is no match for intuition, and it's a big man who'll admit when he's wrong. But it's the little woman who'll make him admit it!

*

Comedians make light of marriage, but it has been proved that married life is healthy. Statistics show that single people die sooner than married folks. So if you're looking for a long life and a slow death, get married!

*

She keeps reminding him of all the things he said he'd do when they got married. But let's face it—who pays any attention to campaign promises?

*

Marriage often broadens a man, but it also has a tendency to make him short.

*

Many a man who looks for the apple of his eye, and marries her, later begins to realize his search was fruitless.

*

Marriage is like a vaccination: Sometimes you get a reaction right from scratch.

*

No matter whom you marry in June, it turns out to be someone else in August.

*

It was the great philosopher Socrates who said: "By all means marry! If you get a good wife you will be very happy; if you get a bad one you will become a philosopher, and that is good for any man."

*

Marriage is often the result of a little twitch in the right eye that develops into oceans of emotions surrounded by an expanse of expense caused by too much squeezing.

*

The man who marries a wisp of a girl is often surprised at the will of the wisp.

*

There are some men who will never forget the day they were married—but they keep trying.

*

Take the average couple as an example. Half the time she's right and the other half he's wrong. He makes the money and she makes the decisions.

*

In marriage, no wife gets what she expected and no husband expected what he's getting.

*

The romance has gone out of marriage when she stops calling him Honey and starts calling him Listen, You.

*

Contrary to the opinion of a lot of folks, there are some men who can honestly say that since the day they were married they have never even looked at another woman. They're completely discouraged!

*

There's many a belle who finds that marriage is just one wringer after another.

*

She used to be his pet lamb. Then they got married, now she's just a little bossy.

*

The ties of matrimony usually follow when a girl collars her man.

*

Before marriage a girl speaks to him with her eyes; afterward it's with her tongue.

*

The best way for a man to find out what a woman thinks of him is to marry her.

*

Many a couple see eye to eye, but there are daggers between them.

*

Marriage is often the result of taking a leap in the dark by the light of the moon.

*

Troubles in marriage often begin when a man is so busy earning his salt that he forgets his sugar.

*

Whether a fellow winds up with a nest egg or a goose egg depends a lot on the kind of chick he married.

*

Marriage is a hard proposition! It takes grit to propose, sand to go through the ceremony and rocks to support a family.

*

Believe it or not, marriage is one sure way of teaching a man that there is a higher power.

*

MARRIAGE: A lesson that teaches a man a lot of things he wouldn't have believed just from hearing.

*

When you see what some girls marry, you realize how they must have hated to work for a living.

*

Some fellows like to brag about the figure of their intended, but after the wedding they often discover that honesty is not always the bust policy.

*

In marriage it's not a sin to tell a lie—it's an impossibility!

*

Married couples can often have pleasant conversations—if the husbands don't start talking back.

*

Something has gone out of marriage when he starts wondering what happened to the girl he married and she starts wondering what happened to the man she didn't.

*

Often a word to the wife is sufficient to start something.

*

Many a man sweeps a girl off her feet—and then goes through life with the broom still in his hands.

*

Marriage is often a lot of little mouths to feed and a big one to listen to.

*

Many an orator has gotten married and lost his voice.

*

A pretty girl may be like a melody, but after you marry her you've got to face the music.

*

Things sort of even themselves up in life. For example, some married men give dictation all day and listen to it all evening.

*

Sometimes marriage is like a game of checkers—a mighty struggle to get into the king row.

*

You can't always judge how expensive a thing is by its price. A marriage license costs only a few bucks.

*

Many a man who doesn't believe in eternal punishment gets married and finds out for himself.

*

When you are married, you never can tell—a lot of little things can happen.

*

Marriage is an institution where a man faces the wedding march for the first time, and faces the music forever after.

*

Before marriage, couples smiled at the lovable eccentricities of each other's relatives. Later they're both convinced they must have married into a family of wild-eyed lunatics.

*

When a man says his wife is gifted, he probably has the bills to prove it.

*

The trouble with marriage is that the couple start out with a king and queen, wind up with a full house, and the husband gets lost in the shuffle.

*

Some of the fellows who used to think that marriages were made in heaven are beginning to lower their opinions.

*

Marriages are made in heaven—but so are thunder and lightning.

*

You always know they're married when she looks at the dresses in the window and he looks at the skirts on the sidewalk.

*

Ever notice how some girls go from "I do" to "You'd better"?

*

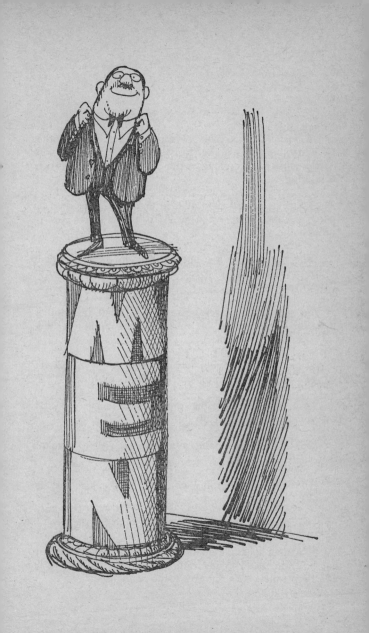

A man's life is twenty years of having his mother ask him where he's going, forty years of having his wife ask the same question and, at the end, having the mourners wondering too.

*

Man has a hard time of it in life! No sooner does he bolt the door against the wolf than the stork flies in through the window.

*

Every man who is a success likes to think he did it all by himself—and his wife just smiles and lets it go at that.

*

To size up the average man, add what his mother thinks of him to what his mother-in-law thinks of him, and then divide by two.

*

There are men who, having once swept a girl off her feet, are now sweeping up the whole apartment.

*

Men have been losing ground ever since the first cave dweller made his club out of soft wood.

*

Up to a certain point a man goes with a woman; after that he's taken.

*

The man who says his wife can't take a joke forgets himself.

*

There's many a rough neck in a stiff collar.

*

If a man looks at another woman it may not mean that he's interested in her. Still, a man doesn't look at a road map unless he's figuring to go someplace.

*

The man who is able to pitch a good line doesn't necessarily have a lot on the ball.

*

After the age of four, a man is never master in his home again.

*

It is an incontrovertible fact that if you give a man plenty of rope, he will get himself all tangled up with some woman.

*

The man who doesn't know his own strength is an easy mark for the girl who knows his weakness.

*

Man is nothing but a cloud of dust, and it takes a woman to settle him.

*

The greatness of many a man is merely the possession of a clever wife.

*

A man-about-town is usually a fool about women.

*

Men have been getting sissier and sissier ever since they quit striking matches on the seat of their pants.

*

A man is a creature who knows what's on the other side of the moon, but can't tell what's in the back of his wife's mind.

*

Somehow or another a man is never happy until something in a skirt comes along and makes him miserable.

*

Indifference in a man is a barrier that few women can handle.

*

Contrary to the fears of alarmists, it's more and more a man's world. Now he's even taken over the kitchen.

*

Some fellows follow the straight and narrow, others are interested in curves.

*

The average man is 39 around the chest, 40 around the waist, 96 around the golf course and a nuisance around the house.

*

When a man has everything that a woman could ask for, she usually does.

*

It's a man's world—until he gets home from the office.

*

Some men may not be handsome but still have loads of charm—which they keep in a number of banks.

*

When men get too big for their britches, it's easy to fill their shoes.

*

Many a man is in the doghouse for biting off more than he can chew.

*

It's when some men are feeling fit as a fiddle that they begin looking around for a female accompanist.

*

We like the man whose impulse it is to say yes much better than the one whose impulse it is to say no. But the trouble is that the former never has anything to lend.

*

Men may have a way with women—but it's seldom their own.

*

By the time a man learns where he stands, his feet hurt.

*

A man gets exuberant over a raise in pay, while his wife keeps calm and collects it.

*

All men are born equal—and spend their life vainly trying to catch up with the women.

*

FACT: Only one perfect man ever existed. He's the guy your wife could have married.

*

The most attractive men are not those with broad, tan shoulders, but the guys with the green backs.

*

Some men have all the sterling qualities every woman wants—good looks, clean habits and spend their money like water.

*

The only man in history who never looked at another woman was named Adam.

*

The ideal man, according to most girls, is the one who is smart enough to make a lot of money, and stupid enough to get married.

*

The man of the hour is the one whose wife told him to wait a minute.

*

The wise man not only lets his wife have the last word, but he's happy when she gets to it.

*

The man who is as busy as a bee may wake up to find his honey missing.

*

No matter how big a man is, he can always fit under a woman's thumb.

*

All men are created equally susceptible to feminine charms.

*

The man who works like a horse usually draws a girl with a beautiful carriage.

*

When a man thinks his wife doesn't understand him, he usually picks a pretty girl for an interpreter.

*

If you want to hear a man growl like a bear, just clean out his den.

*

Through the ages man has progressed to the point where he walks upright—but his eyes still swing from limb to limb.

*

There are a powerful lot of strings in a man's life: apron, heart, purse and harp.

*

A man is never so weak as when a pretty girl is telling him how strong he is.

*

An average man is one who isn't as good as his wife thought he was before she married him—or as bad as she thinks he is afterward.

*

The only bright spots in some men's lives are on the seats of their pants.

*

The masculine gesture most admired by women is probably that of reaching for a checkbook.

*

After man came woman—and she's still in the race.

*

Boys will be boys—and so will middle-aged men at smokers.

*

All the average man asks for in life is a little *peach* and quiet.

*

It doesn't matter whether a man is a man or a mouse; in the end some cat gets him anyway.

*

ADVICE TO GIRLS: Getting a man in his twenties is as easy as throwing a rope around the neck of a work horse, but in his thirties, it's like lassoing a bronco.

*

The main reason the average man hates to see his wife go home to her mother is that she might bring the old girl back with her.

*

MAN: His ingenuity in getting out of tight corners is exceeded only by his dumbness in getting into them.

*

By the time a man can read a woman like a book, he's too old to start a library.

*

Many a man with a model wife often becomes interested in inspecting the later models.

*

Nothing makes a man go places like a woman who likes to.

*

Some men, like tea, never know their real strength until they get in hot water.

*

Money is funny. You have to be dead to get your face on it, but very much alive to get your hands on it.

*

The hardest thing to explain to the wife about money matters is that money matters.

*

Maybe you can't take it with you when you go, but there are darned few places you can go without it.

*

We've often heard tell that a dog is a man's best friend; but most of us have more faith in the buck.

*

Money may not be everything, but it's sure a great consolation until you have everything.

*

They tell us that money is filthy, but a little of it will sure buy a heap of disinfectant.

*

It takes the long green to show up a man's real colors.

*

WEALTH: A curse when the neighbors have it.

*

Most of us have two chances of becoming wealthy— slim and none.

*

Financial success is a wonderful thing. You meet such interesting relatives.

*

A man with a lot of money may be a bad egg, but folks seldom take offense until he's broke.

*

Pretending to be rich keeps a lot of us mighty poor.

*

There are no idle rich. They're all kept busy dodging people who want some of it.

*

There are three faithful friends: an old wife, an old dog and ready money.

*

The real trouble with money is that you can't use it more than once.

*

It never did bother us too much to see our friends and acquaintances have more money than we have, but what drives us crazy is how they do it.

*

Cold cash makes people warm up to you.

*

The best way to jingle coins in your pocket is to shake a leg.

*

When it comes to making money, most men have to hand it to a woman.

*

Money can't go to heaven, but it can do some heavenly things here on earth.

*

A fellow's money goes just as far as ever—from him to his wife.

*

Some wives are not exactly hungry for money, but on payday the old man puts his paycheck on the table and jumps back.

*

A lot of folks get a bad case of the blues when they've got a shortage of the green.

*

They call it legal tender,
That green and crackling stuff—
It's tender when you have it,
But when you don't, it's tough.

*

FACT: There is no better companion than a fat wallet.

*

Money may not be everything in life, but it sure is giving whatever is in first place a good race.

*

Things always look greener in the other fellow's wallet.

*

Wealth may not bring happiness, but it would seem nice to try a small sample anyway.

*

The difference between a rich man and the rest of us is that, while he tries to break 90, we're satisfied if we can break even.

*

Fortune may smile on some, but for the rest of us she just laughs.

*

Those who have money have trouble about it—
Those who have none have trouble without it.

*

Maybe the reason that money is referred to as "jack" is because the "queen" takes it.

*

Money may not buy peace at home, but it'll negotiate a darn nice armistice.

*

FRUSTRATION: When you feel money on all sides of you, but can't get your hands on any part of it.

*

When you're in the chips, it's much easier to be chipper.

*

Money won't buy love, but it'll sure put a fellow in a mighty good bargaining position.

*

Our private opinion is that a lot of billfolds these days seem to have a hollow sound.

*

Today money passes through our hands so fast it sounds like a tobacco auctioneer.

*

If it's true that the love of money is the root of all evil, there's a lot of us shouting, "Shoot the roots to me, Toots."

*

Did you ever notice that when you have a roll of that "filthy lucre," there are a lot of folks anxious to take you to the cleaners?

*

The best way to be known as the meanest man in town is to have more money than your neighbors.

*

When a man is poor he leads a simple life. When he is rich, the doctor orders it.

*

The world's wealthiest man says he doesn't know precisely how rich he is. It's the same with the rest of us: We think we're doing pretty well and then the water heater breaks down.

*

There's nothing that counts as much as money—except Scotch and women. But you need money for them too.

*

Nothing lures the female gender like stacks of legal tender.

*

When it comes to money there are two kinds of people, the earners and the spenders—more popularly known as husbands and wives.

*

The way we figure, anyone who has no money in his purse should have honey on his tongue.

*

FACT: Some fellows are well-to-do because others found them hard to do.

*

Having the "sugar" is always a big help toward having a sweet disposition.

*

The skin we love to touch is the frog skin.

*

Money is funny. Men get their pictures on it and woman gets their hands on it.

*

Few people are allergic to the long green.

*

A little man never looks so big to the world as when he is well entrenched in a bag of money.

*

If you're looking for a note of harmony that will settle most disputes, it's "dough."

*

Those who have it these days are not speaking very loudly, lest the tax collector hear it and becomes suspicious.

*

If you have an idea that your youngsters don't know the value of money, try giving them a penny.

*

Don't worry about an occasional bit of bad publicity concerning the dollar. Bankers report that after centuries of sneers, knocks and abuse, money is more in demand than ever.

*

There are more important things in life than money, but they won't go out with you when you're broke.

*

One thing nice about money is that the color of it never clashes with anything you're wearing.

*

It may be hard for a wealthy man to enter the kingdom of heaven, but it sure is easy for him to get on the board of trustees of his church.

*

Those of us who can't see where our money is going these days just can't see fast-moving objects.

*

Cheer up! The less money you have, the more there is to get.

*

Any time anyone tells you that a hunk of long green isn't everything, well, they've never attended a suit contesting a will.

*

Taking it with you isn't so important. The problem is to make it last until you're ready to go.

*

Someone has figured out that, on the average, each dollar in circulation is spent every twenty days. Maybe so, but no buck in our house stays that long.

*

MONEY: The golden key that opens many a stubborn lock.

*

MOTHERS-IN-LAW

MOTHER-IN-LAW: A puzzle with cross words.

*

In some sections of Africa it is the custom for a husband to stand a respectful distance away when addressing his mother-in-law. Over here, we don't call it a custom—we call it plain old safety first.

*

It's an even bet as to which is colder,
A wife's feet or her mother's shoulder.

*

Until they met their mother-in-law, a lot of fellows never realized that there was a Mrs. Scrooge.

*

Many a wife, you may have noticed, has a nice chin —and as for her mother, that goes double.

*

You've got to believe that some mothers-in-law are really magicians, after you see the daughters they've palmed off on unsuspecting guys.

*

A statistical expert says that only one person in every 200,000 is ever struck by lightning. Well, if any of the other 199,999 ever become bored with life, they can always get practically the same exhilarating effect by "sassing" their mother-in-law.

*

When a mother-in-law minds her own business it doesn't necessarily mean she has good sense. She may be deaf.

*

All I can say is that the guy who wrote "Home, Sweet Home" never lived with his mother-in-law.

*

Some men refrain from telling mother-in-law jokes. You know why? There's absolutely nothing funny about a mother-in-law.

*

If you don't believe in the theory of evolution, how do you account for your mother-in-law?

*

MOTHER-IN-LAW: An accessory after the pact!

*

Few mistakes can be made by a mother-in-law who is willing to baby-sit.

*

There must be some significance in the fact that when a man tells his wife to "go to the devil," she usually goes straight home to her mother.

*

We don't think it's right for a fellow to blame his wife for everything that goes wrong. After all, what can he expect from a girl that was raised by his mother-in-law?

*

Nothing improves a wife's cooking as much as a visit from her mother-in-law.

*

You seldom find a mother-in-law who is a laughing mater.

*

When a mother-in-law rules the roost, the rooster cackles—or runs to another.

*

The Constitution explicitly states that a man cannot be placed in double jeopardy. How come, then, that the laws fail to protect him against his mother-in-law moving in on him?

*

Some mothers-in-law have mouths like a hamburger stand—open day and night.

*

Some fellows begin to suspect their mother-in-law's low opinion of them when they receive a gift of towels marked "Hers" and "Its."

*

Many a man has endured a conference with two dictators—his wife and his mother-in-law.

*

A "blessed event" in some homes is when the mother-in-law goes to her own home.

*

QUESTION: What is faster than a mother-in-law's tongue going through her son-in-law's business?

*

They say every woman has her price. Well, a lot of fellows have a mother-in-law they'll let you have real cheap.

*

Some couples have a perfect union—until her mother becomes the shop steward.

*

We have nothing against mothers-in-law, generally speaking—except that they are generally speaking.

*

Harmony between a daughter-in-law and a mother-in-law can often be gauged by the number of recipes each uses from the other's files.

*

Politics

Politics helps to simplify history. Anything bad that happens during an administration, they inherited. Anything good, they invented.

*

The political bee buzzes loudest around the candidates for office, but it's usually the public that gets stung.

*

A political job may not take much know-how, but it sure takes a lot of know-who.

*

Political campaigns teach us that not all people who stretch the facts are fishermen and golfers.

*

Politicians may promise a chicken in every pot, but too often it's the taxpayer's goose that's cooked.

*

In politics, appointing a committee doesn't solve the problem, but it gets everybody home in time for dinner.

*

FACT: We took the country away from the Indians, who scalped us, and gave it to the politicians, who skin us.

*

Politics is the fine art of passing the buck—after passing the hat.

*

Some politicians repair their fences by hedging.

*

Old-time politicians remember when they could buy a whole ward for what a few seconds on TV cost today.

*

There are two sides to every question, but some of the questions windily debated by politicians are like bass drums: After you listen to both sides, you still haven't heard much.

*

Politics differs from poker. In politics you play first and cut afterward.

*

The hand-shaking done by Presidential candidates provides enough energy to milk all the taxpayers for the next four years.

*

Politics is like milking a cow. A lot can be accomplished with a little pull.

*

If you would like to know what kind of a life your ancestors lived, just try running for public office and your opponents will tell you.

*

No matter how often a politician runs for office, he seldom gets winded.

*

Love, sausage, hash and the ways of the average politician are the mysteries of life.

*

When women go into politics it's the old man who has to swing the dish rag and tend to the butt end of the baby.

*

Politicians, like poor relatives, are seen only when they need help.

*

A skillful politician is one who can stand up and rock the boat, and then make you believe he is the one who can save you in a storm.

*

Some candidates concede that their critics may be right when they call them a one-issue man. In this case, though, the one issue is getting elected.

*

By the end of any political campaign, few stones will be left unturned or unflung.

*

Adding to the already serious problem of air pollution is the hot air of our politicians.

*

Ever notice that when politicians are thrown out of office, they turn to writing books about their experiences? It's a case of perish, then publish.

*

Politics is the art of making yourself popular with the people by giving them grants out of their own money.

*

The pollsters complain that one segment of the American public always plays them a dirty trick—the "undecideds" who finally make up their minds.

*

The political speeches we usually hear are quite amazing, considering they come from an alphabet of only twenty-six letters.

*

It used to be that guinea pigs multiplied the fastest. Then along came the government job holders.

*

Some candidates who kissed babies during the campaign are crying harder after the election than the babies ever did.

*

Some politicians may claim to be men of few words, but they sure keep them mighty busy.

*

Candidates who run with one foot pointed North and the other pointed South soon get mighty hard to track.

*

The wonderful thing about being a politician is that your wife never knocks you in public.

*

Politics is like kissing—you don't have to be good at it.

*

How come those who claim the country is ruined are trying so hard to get control of the wreck?

*

Candidates are always telling us how bright we look. Well, for gosh sakes, why shouldn't we look bright? Those birds have sure cleaned us plenty!

*

There is only one thing that can make people do and say more foolish things than love can, and that's politics.

*

The pity of politics is that we can never give the outs their innings without giving the ins their outing.

*

POLITICAL PLATFORM: A preach of promise.

*

Seems to us that a politician is a fellow who sings "The Star-Spangled Banner" before election and "To Each His Own" after he's been elected.

*

A lot of politicians these days gas their audiences instead of electrifying them.

*

When some of our politicians start to speak, the night has a thousand "I"s.

*

When a politician says the nation is due for a re-awakening, it means he is running for office.

*

POLITICAL OPTIMIST: A fellow who can make sweet pink lemonade out of the bitter yellow fruit his opponents hand him.

*

Choosing a candidate is a lot like finding a baby-sitter. If you can't get the one you want, you've got to take what you can get.

*

Take a look at your tax bills and you'll stop calling them "cheap" politicians.

*

Some politicians haven't made up their mind whether to run for another term of office or not, but they're sitting by an open window so they can hear the voice of the people, and letting one arm hang out in case anybody wants to twist it.

*

All through the campaign some candidates kept bragging that they were not politicians, and the election returns proved they were right.

*

The way we figure, beware of the candidates who promote pie in the sky. They plan to use your dough.

*

We find that when the candidates orate about the great unfinished task, it means they are willing to stay on the payroll.

*

If you would be successful in politics, build your fences only high enough to be comfortably straddled.

*

There's nothing that can equal the tenderness of a hard-boiled egg who is scrambling for reelection.

*

If you can fool most of the people most of the time, you're a successful politician.

*

The politician who is always trying to create a sensation soon gets so that he can't even create a disturbance.

*

Politics is about the only thing you can get a stomach-ful of, at the old rates.

*

POLITICIAN: A man who keeps his ear to the ground, and his hand in the taxpayer's pocket.

*

The politician who is expecting the office to seek the man always makes sure that his phone number is well publicized.

*

LAME DUCK: A politician who is in the process of becoming a cooked goose.

*

The more you listen to political speeches, the more you realize that this is indeed the Land of Promise.

*

A politician is a man of soft words, free speech, broken promises—and the public's most expensive luxury.

*

That feeling of looseness around the waist is a wonderful thing when a fellow is trying to lose a few pounds. Of course, he can get the same feeling by buying shorts two sizes too big.

*

A woman may believe that faith will move mountains, but she knows doggone well it'll never remove surplus fat.

*

Some women reduce and reduce, but never become a bargain.

*

A girl with an hourglass figure rates a second look any day.

*

When some men have a weight problem, it's because the wife is grouchy when she's taking it off, and grouchier when she's putting it on.

*

Advice to men over forty: Keep an open mind and a closed refrigerator.

*

When a girl starts reducing, the first thing she loses is her temper.

*

Hips spring eternal as a female pest.

*

Be it ever so humble, there's no shape like your own! So sneak a peek at your physique and if it's not as sleek as you think it should be, maybe you'd better start reshaping. Or, like the man said, "Trim your torso!"

*

Fat folks know that the reducing business is still being done on a large scale.

*

The way we figure, the worst kind of reducing pill is the one who keeps telling you how he did it.

*

Whenever a man notices his wife performing some strange and unusual contortions, there's really no need for him to worry. She may just be doing her seven thinning stretches.

*

It's ironic that when a girl starves herself until she gets her desired weight back, every fellow she knows wants to take her out to dinner.

*

What reduces some reducers is the fretting over what they're supposed to eat.

*

Reducing is the Battle of the Bulge.

*

If a fellow really wants to lose a few pounds, all he has to do is persuade his wife to go on a reducing diet. That should do the trick!

*

The easiest way to get rid of weight
Is to leave it on the plate.

*

Girls who keep their figure have better chances of fellows calling their number.

*

To feel fit as a fiddle
Trim your middle.

*

There are a lot of women who spend a good hunk of money trying to slenderize, but all they succeed in reducing is the old man's bankroll.

*

The trouble with reducing pills is that they usually reduce our wallet more than they do our weight.

*

Buy a book on reducing and in no time at all you'll realize—you've lost the price of the book.

*

It's the desire to reduce that keeps a lot of girls from eating between snacks.

*

What is responsible for a lot of us going on a reducing diet isn't so much our own desire or the orders of our doctor as it is the grocer, the butcher and the baker. After all, the prices they charge is enough to take the starch out of anybody.

*

Those girls who leap from one reducing gimmick to another must be a group of hipochondriacs.

*

It's hard to reduce expenses—or expanses.

*

A reducing diet is the only thing that's usually forgotten faster than a New Year's resolution.

*

We starve and suffer, but bless our soul—
Our waistline's still beyond our control.

*

FACT: You can't reduce by just talking about it; you've got to keep your mouth shut.

*

The only sure way to reduce is to set the bathroom scale in front of the refrigerator.

*

Any time a man loses as much as a hundred pounds or so by exercising, that's what we call pot luck.

*

No matter how much some men lose, they still have a big head.

*

Eating your own words is good for reducing your ego.

*

Reducing classes for women are what keep wives bending and husbands broke.

*

When a girl slims down, it sure takes a weight off her mind.

*

After some of these fourteen-day diets, about all that is lost is two weeks.

*

In our estimation, the best way to lose those extra pounds is to eat a lot of food. If you do, you'll get lazy; if you're lazy, you won't want to work; if you don't work, how can you earn any money?; and if you have no money, you can't buy food, and if you can't buy food, you won't be able to eat—and if you don't eat, brother, you'll lose plenty of weight!

*

FACT: Before the reducing salons begin to slenderize you, they slenderize your wallet.

*

Two of the most difficult things for us to learn is that a person can improve his financial condition by spending less, and his physical condition by eating less.

*

The various reducing juices, powders and diets are said to be delicious. But what's the merit in losing weight unless you suffer a bit?

*

These professional reducers are usually rolling in dough,
But their living is easy and grand.
They starve all the girls, but as for themselves,
They live off the fat of the land.

*

I've done everything to lose weight. For six months I sweated on a rowing machine. Even then I didn't lose any weight—but I got awfully seasick.

*

To a lot of us, reducing is nothing more than wishful shrinking.

*

MASSEUSE: An expert on fats and figures.

*

One crying need of humanity is a reducing diet for fatheads.

*

An ounce of prevention is worth hours of exercise in order to lose a pound.

*

A lot of girls are wearing reducing stockings for their legs. In fact, you can hardly recognize the old joints.

*

If women could reduce by exercising their vocal chords, what a gang of thin women we'd have!

*

The best reducing exercise known to date is to move the head slowly from side to side when offered second helpings.

*

There's nothing that reduces a man's bankroll like a large-economy-size blonde.

*

Figures show that there has been quite an increase in the sale of foundation garments.

*

Some folks ride a bike to reduce—and fall off quite a bit.

*

The first thing a man has to do before he can reduce by going on a diet is to build up his will power until it is stronger than his appetite.

*

Most of us are good losers when it comes to reducing.

*

A girl will go to any length to change her width.

*

The best things in life are free, according to a well-known song, but just let our politicians hear about that and they won't be free for long—they'll be taxed!

*

The reason for the expression "cool million" is that, after taxes, the balance ain't so hot.

*

To the tax assessor, be they ever so humble there's no place like homes.

*

If the time ever comes when you feel you'd like to be alone without a friend in the world, try visiting the tax review board for a reduction on your home assessment.

*

The average American taxpayer thinks he has his nose to the grindstone when really he has his back to the wall.

*

Nothing is certain but death and taxes, and each gets you in a hole.

*

One hopeful note on hidden taxes is that there can't be many more places to hide them.

*

When the government talks about getting a new source of revenue, it always comes back to the same place—the taxpayer.

*

No matter what the government thinks of us, you have to admit we have what it takes.

*

While it seems silly to mention it now, this country was founded as a protest against taxation.

*

Modern man pays a luxury tax on his billfold, an income tax on the stuff he puts into it, and a sales tax every time he takes anything out of it.

*

There is this to be said about the average taxpayer: He's alive and kicking.

*

Every time Congress sets out to cut expenses, the knife slips and trims the taxpayers.

*

The way taxes are, very few girls get the chance anymore to marry for money.

*

Between high taxes and high prices, we're always cleaned and pressed.

*

After the average taxpayer has finished paying a few hundred taxes—hidden as well as out in the open—he usually feels bled, white and blue.

*

Whether a fellow tries to be a fox or a lamb, when it's taxpaying time he ends up being the goat.

*

There's one consolation about life and taxes: When you're through with one, you're through with the other.

*

Never favor a "temporary" tax unless you can afford to pay it permanently.

*

Hidden taxes, like the hidden pin in a new shirt, eventually let you know they are there.

*

The two sneakiest words in the English language are "plus tax."

*

Only taxes and strapless evening gowns seem to defy the laws of gravity.

*

Adam had no clothes to buy and no taxes to pay. That's why the Garden of Eden was called Paradise.

*

There are plenty of tax loopholes to go around, but the trouble is that most of us are too fatheaded to squeeze through them.

*

These days all you have to do to find out where your money goes is to study geography.

*

Congress puts a big tax on liquor and then raises other taxes that drive people to drink.

*

How are you managing the tax problem at your home? At ours, we're using the lay-awake plan.

*

When it comes to the matter of tax reduction, never was so little waited for by so many.

*

The main difference between General Custer's time and today is that the Indians scalped their victims with axes, while Uncle Sam does it with taxes.

*

They say you can't take it with you, but with taxes as they are, how far can you go without it?

*

If Patrick Henry had known what taxation with representation was like, he would have kept his mouth shut.

*

The only think left to tax is the wolf at the door.

*

Trying to get taxes reduced is about as easy to do as pulling off a corn plaster without removing the shoe.

*

TAXES: A bitter bill to swallow.

*

If the cost of living continues to rise, a lot of taxpayers will be either delinquent or hungry.

*

Do you suppose the sales tax was invented so that pennies wouldn't feel lonesome?

*

Nothing distributes wealth like taxation and a large family.

*

The man who says that at least it doesn't cost anything to laugh apparently hasn't heard of the amusement tax.

*

There's one thing to be said in favor of the "pay-as-you-go" plan. You don't get mad all at once. It's spread out!

*

The huge national debt our younger generation will inherit should keep them from one indulgence—ancestor worship.

*

When it comes time for the meek to inherit the earth, the taxes will probably be so high they won't take it.

*

The average taxpayer no longer feels that Congress will let him down; he just hopes that Congress will let him up.

*

The word "tax" comes from the Latin word *taxare*, which means "to touch sharply." No further comment needed, is there?

*

The tax collector must love poor people! He's creating so many of them.

*

Money talks, but all it talks about is taxes.

*

Some biologist once said that man's jaw is receding. Well, no wonder, what with the way he's been taking it on the chin for years.

*

Making money is getting to be like bees making honey. You can make it, but they won't let you keep it.

*

Something's going to slip sooner or later. The world is standing on Uncle Sam's shoulders, Uncle Sam is standing on the American taxpayer's back—and the American taxpayer is standing on the ragged edge.

*

The only thing higher than taxes these days is a dope addict.

*

Once a fool and his money were soon parted, but today the tax bureaus make no distinction.

*

It's still death and taxes, but one is taking the sting out of the other.

*

Some of us never worry about not being able to take it with us. What little we have left isn't worth carrying.

*

There's even a new tax on miracle drugs! You still get the drugs at the old rate, but they tax you on the miracles.

*

It's getting to the point where our youngsters have to be educated to realize that "damn" and "taxes" are two different words.

*

Everything has to be taxed—even our patience.

*

Taxes are what we pay to keep the government running—so that it can keep us running to pay taxes.

*

Why is it the taxpayer is the only "varmint" expected to yield a pelt every year?

*

It's been said there are better days ahead, but the tax boys won't let you get far enough ahead to find them.

*

Asking the boss for a raise these days is a patriotic duty, as Uncle Sam needs the additional tax on your salary.

*

Wonder if the tax collectors are trying to convince us that money isn't everything?

*

Atlas was a weakling compared to the modern taxpayer.

*

huehnengarth

We revolted against taxation without representation, and got taxation without relaxation.

*

A taxpayer is a guy who works hard to save a little out of his paycheck—and the politician is a guy who is glad of it.

*

The difference between direct taxes and indirect taxes is about the same as your wife asking you for a bit of change and then going through your pockets when you're asleep.

*

Wouldn't it be wonderful if we could all raise taxes as easily as Congress does?

*

There isn't much chance for a tax reduction as long as our politicians are afflicted with spendicitis.

*

Some Congressman is supposed to have said: "We mustn't kill the taxpayer who lays the golden egg." Well, we've got news for whoever said that. The taxpayer doesn't lay those golden eggs; the various governments, local, state and federal, extract them through an operation that's comparable to a Caesarean section!

*

It's been said that the easiest way to get into a taxpayer's pocket is to scare the pants off him.

*

Speaking of taxes, never have so few taken so many for so much.

*

If they ever tax politicians and other speakers on their chatter, some folks are going to get a mighty big gas bill.

*

If taxes continue to soar, we're going to have to work like a dog to live like one.

*

Among those who listen to money talk these days are tax collectors.

*

In these days there is no such thing as a small tax-payer.

*

No matter in which direction a tax is hurled, it always hits the ultimate consumer.

*

Have you noticed how all the taxpayers are looking for a break in the levy?

*

It's been said there is nothing surer than death and taxes, but the way things are today, the average citizen spends a lot of his time and energy trying to postpone the former and dodge the latter.

*

Any time a taxpayer notes in the news that the federal government is asking for certain appropriations for planned new projects, he may ask: "Where is all that money coming from?" But you know as well as I do that he has his suspicions.

*

Reducing taxes is sometimes like the weather. Every-body, including politicians, talk about it. Period.

*

It's true that we can't take it with us, but the way taxes are today, we can't even afford to go.

*

It isn't how hard it is for a wealthy man to enter the kingdom of heaven that concerns the majority of us—it's how hard it is for the average poor taxpayer to stay on earth.

*

Of all the sad words of tongue or pen, the saddest are: "Those darned taxes have been raised again!"

*

Seems like the only transaction that isn't taxed these days is laying up a treasure in heaven.

*

Ever notice how taxes are a lot like rosebushes? The more thay are pruned the higher they grow.

*

Providence may temper the wind to the shorn lamb, but the fleeced taxpayer isn't so lucky.

*

One of the most irritating blows below the belt is the tax on restaurant meals.

*

With estate and inheritance taxes what they are, the happiest mourner at a rich man's funeral is his Uncle Sam.

*

There was a time when only Washington's face was on our dollar bills—now Washington's hands are on it.

*

All these taxes have taught the majority of us a lesson. At least we know how a cow feels toward a milking machine.

*

Someone once said that cows are sometimes bitter and neurotic. Well, maybe they're like a lot of taxpayers—they get tired of being milked.

*

It's true that this country was founded to avoid taxation. But, brother, our founding forefathers should take a look now!

*

Did you know that you can get a government bulletin on almost every subject—except curbing government expenses?

*

There's only one trouble with saving for a rainy day. Some tax collector is sure to come along and soak you.

*

Don't worry too much about not taking it with you. In one place you wouldn't need it, and in the other you couldn't use it.

*

When it comes to knocking down a big salary, you just can't beat the government.

*

The world hasn't been inherited by the meek, but it sure is being supported by a lot of them.

*

Life nowadays is certainly taxing.

*

Statisticians tell us that the average American now pays more in taxes than he does for food. Could be, but all we have to say is that paying taxes isn't nearly as much fun as eating.

*

Save your pennies, and the sales tax will take care of them.

*

The wealthy folks of today can probably be credited with a lot of hard work, a little luck and a doggone smart tax expert.

*

Someone once said that folks in the United States are the cleanest people in the world. Well, why shouldn't we be clean? Look at the way the taxpayers have been taken to the cleaners.

*

If money is the root of all evil, as we've been taught, the average taxpayer needn't worry too much about the hereafter.

*

ADVICE: Never overtax yourself—the government will do it for you.

*

Anyone who believes he hasn't a dependent on earth must think the government is out of this world.

*

This *is* the land of opportunity! Where else could you make enough to pay so many different taxes?

*

Ever notice how men of untold wealth shudder whenever they see an envelope from the Treasury Department?

*

There are thousands of hidden taxes these days, but nary a place where the taxpayer can hide.

*

Don't worry too much about the coming generation being soft. It'll harden them up when they realize the tremendous debt they'll have to pay off.

*

Look at it this way: If you didn't have to pay out all that money in taxes, you'd probably just go out and spend it anyway.

*

Congress passes bills; taxpayers pay them.

*

In the tax program it's a great deal safer to soak the poor and the middle class because they can't afford to hire expensive lawyers.

*

Those of us who pay as we go aren't doing very much going.

*

When the average man looks at what he has left after paying his various taxes, he begins to realize that Social Security may have some real meaning for him after all.

*

If all the tax dollars collected in one year were laid end to end—a lot of us would sure welcome a big wind.

*

It's the same old routine every year. We work 365 days like the very devil just to make it, and about the time we're ready to start eating steady-like, the government steps in and takes it.

*

Television may be a great entertainment vehicle, but some of the programs sure take the public for a ride.

*

Many a TV program would have a happier ending if we just had the energy to get up and turn it off sooner.

*

Let's face it. Television has opened many a door—mostly on refrigerators.

*

COMMERCIAL TRAVELER: One who takes a trip to the bathroom or the refrigerator during the sponsor's message.

*

Television commercials are those brief few moments when a man pays attention to his wife—and his kidneys.

*

TV commercials may be a bore, but just think how many peddlers they keep from your door.

*

The difference between radio and TV is that radio wakes folks up in the morning, and TV puts them to sleep at night.

*

What with football, baseball, basketball and track stars selling mouthwashes, deodorants, after-shave lotions and scented shaving creams on TV, America must have the sweetest-smelling athletes of all time!

*

Many of the old-timers can remember the days before radio and TV, when only hogs produced ham and only chickens laid eggs.

*

Every now and then somebody says something flattering about TV programs. The other day a critic said that most of them are mediocre.

*

TV has gone haywire! Comedians insist on giving us humor with a message. And politicians give us messages with humor. Unfortunately, the second group is funnier than the first.

*

FACT: We didn't realize how lucky we were during the golden age of radio, before there was television. Think of it—all those years we listened to radio and nobody invented the radio dinner.

*

Indirectly, slowly and to a small degree, television is becoming educational. It's driving people to reading books.

*

Personally, I think TV is still in its infancy. Some of the shows sure could use a change.

*

With all these commercials on television, it makes a parent feel kind of silly punishing a child for lying.

*

TV ratings are arrived at by checking a small sample group, and then multiplying their preferences by an awfully big number.

*

TV SPECIAL: A program that comes on instead of the one you stayed home to see.

*

Ordinarily a cold lasts about five days, but a man can get back to the office sooner than that if treated with a diet of daytime television.

*

Some folks have been apprehensive about sending our TV programs abroad. They feel it might damage the American image. Well, in our private opinion it will do just the opposite. It'll impress the world with what a tough, dedicated, persistent people we are to sit through all that stuff.

*

TELEVISION: What makes your pants wear out before your shoes.

*

High on the list of expendables are the TV boys who read commercials as though they were trying to communicate a secret to someone at the bottom of a deep rain barrel.

*

That four-alarm voice on the TV commercials convinces us of one thing: The sponsor knows darn well that we've gone to the kitchen for something to eat.

*

TV keeps advertising a "man's" deodorant. Well, all we have to say is, if that's the only way the girls can tell, forget it!

*

TV has a lot of first-grade comedy in it. The only trouble is that the audience has gone beyond the first grade.

*

Did you ever get the feeling, while viewing some of the old reruns on television, that it's just another way of saying: "The evil men do often lives after them"?

*

DAYTIME TV WESTERNS: Saddle soap operas.

*

Another wonderful thing about television is that they even have people to laugh at the jokes for you.

*

No moron is justified in concluding that life holds no hope for him so long as there are singing commercials to be written.

*

Who says we never get a second chance in this life? Now we can see all the movies we've missed since way back when.

*

TV MOVIES: The story of a beautiful love that comes to a tragic end after getting entangled with a dozen or more commercials.

*

Television makes it possible to fall asleep while listening to a bore without insulting him.

*

The difference between radio and TV is that on radio you wonder what the audience is laughing at; on TV you wonder why.

*

Those girl weather forecasters on TV shouldn't wear plunging necklines. It's confusing when they talk about cold fronts.

*

TV SPONSOR: One who watches the commercials and goes to the refrigerator during the show.

*

Believe it or not, TV has even changed our eating habits. Do you realize that 60 million calories are consumed during every station break?

*

Personally, we're in favor of daytime TV. It keeps a lot of women at home who might otherwise be driving.

*

T.V.

Perhaps vaudeville, too, has nine lives. It has been killed by the stage, the screen and by radio, and now it's being murdered by television.

*

After listening to radio and television news commentators all day, you know that no matter what happens, you've been warned.

*

TV is a strange medium. Some sponsors hire men on horseback to help them sell automobiles.

*

TV has brought a lot of new things into the home—sporting events, operas, plays, movies and repairmen.

*

The big problem of TV program directors is how to fit seventeen one-minute commercials into a fifteen-minute show.

*

The reason for the popularity of westerns with city folks is obvious. Where but in a western can they see one hundred feet of land without a traffic light or a parking meter?

*

The trouble with TV situation comedies is too much situation, not enough comedy.

*

Women prefer to watch other women on TV. It's the only time a housewife can make remarks to another woman's face about her figure without getting a lot of back talk.

*

The marvels of modern communication is that we can hear the same news bulletins all day long.

*

The real thrill of watching a panel discussion on TV is when the guy who has been smoking a pipe and looking wise says something.

*

How did they ever sell soap, toothpaste, beauty aids, automobiles or beer before TV came along?

*

If TV programs don't improve, husbands may go back to listening to their wives.

*

Television is remarkable. The same set that puts you to sleep keeps the neighbors awake.

*

FACT: The only time some families get together for a talk these days is around the refrigerator during TV commercials.

*

If the cigarette commercials on TV were a millimeter shorter, they might not sound nearly so silly.

*

We've got to admit that at times television commercials are really amazing. They make it possible for an ordinary citizen in any part of the country to see a talented actor in Hollywood suffering from acid indigestion.

*

If you think TV is bad now, you ought to go to the movies and see what it's going to be twenty years from now.

*

A lot of old TV programs are going off the air and new ones are replacing them. But how can you tell?

*

Something a lot of folks would like to see advertised on television is an effective remedy for a pain in the neck brought on by blatant and irritating commercials.

*

After studying some of the comics, I've come to the conclusion that the best thing on TV this season will be the little knob that shuts it off.

*

There's always something. No sooner did we get TB under control than we get TV comedians.

*

If a TV comedian wants to keep his wits about him, he'd better pay them well.

*

In the theater it took years for the public to get tired of seeing a performer. On TV he can accomplish the same thing in a single evening.

*

TV COMMERCIAL: The pause that depresses.

*

Commercials on TV are what make you flip the dials so you won't flip your head.

*

I suspect the reason television is called a medium is because so little of it is either rare or well-done.

*

SPONSOR: Anyone courageous enough to admit responsibility for the program.

*

Our private opinion is that stations which feature those old movies should start each day with a prayer. For example, "Forgive us our cinemas."

*

The way we figure, TV permits a man to sit in his own living room and watch any show his wife approves.

*

Advertisers are supposed to know their business, but we still doubt if people can be irritated into buying their products.

*

The good die young was never intended for TV jokes.

*

The minutemen of today are the guys who can make it to the refrigerator and back for a can of beer and a sandwich during a commercial.

*

Many a husband comes home from work with the fond hope that the kitchen stove will be as warm as the TV set.

*

One thing we have to say in favor of some television comedians is that they've just about replaced the sleeping pill.

*

Indians used to broadcast messages by holding a wet blanket over a fire. Now that we've got TV, we get a chance to see the wet blanket in person.

*

There's a lot of money to be made in television; ask any repairman.

*

With a live audience, if a joke is funny they laugh; if it isn't they don't. On TV, when you watch some shows you don't know whether the audience likes the comedian or he just has a good sound man.

*

The only thing that can be said in favor of the commercial is that it's that part of the show in which nobody gets knifed, hanged, choked or shot.

*

If you think germ warfare has been outlawed, you just haven't kept up with television commercials.

*

The trouble with those TV westerns is that they're all alike. The guy wears a .45 gun and the girl wears a 38 sweater.

*

Folks who say that they have half a mind to sit down and watch TV are probably perfectly equipped.

*

TV is really remarkable. It has taken a whole generation of American kids and changed them from an irresistible force to immovable objects.

*

Give TV credit. In a single evening you can learn that all soap powders, cigarettes, beauty creams, gasolines and drain cleaners are infinitely better than all others.

*

Ten percent of the corn presented on TV would be enough to feed the starving people of the world—if they could digest it.

*

TV: Where old movies go to die.

*

These women! How they change once they get a man hooked! Put a "Mrs." in front of a woman's name and it's just like giving a cat its own fish market.

*

Why is it that when a husband comes home late his wife always wants to know where he's been before she tells him where to go?

*

We talk a lot about equality of the sexes, but who ever heard of a housewife going on a pension?

*

When a man's wife has fire in her eyes, then it's cause for alarm.

*

The two greatest crosses the average wife has to bear in this world are a stingy husband and a tight girdle.

*

If King Solomon had so many wives, it probably was because he wanted one in good humor when he came home.

*

When a wife starts wearing the pants in the family, the husband usually shops around for a new skirt.

*

There are two kinds of wives—those who have husbands with money, and those who merely act as if they have.

*

The modern wife is one who puts off today what her husband can do over the weekend.

*

We are living in an age of big spenders—one of whom may be your wife.

*

LEISURE: The two minutes' rest a man gets while his wife is thinking up something for him to do.

*

Many a man, when he sees the bundles his wife brings home, wishes he hadn't married that cute little package.

*

234

When a woman isn't boss of the house, that house is probably still under construction.

*

Observation will disclose that when a wife butters up her husband, she's about to put the bite on him.

*

Many a man loses his balance when his wife goes shopping.

*

There's nothing so pleasing to a wife as to see her husband's old flame with wrinkles and a double chin.

*

Wives are treasures, but some men are sorry they ever dug them up.

*

Ever notice that a wife and an old maid have one thing in common? They're always thinking of the men they could have married.

*

You've got to hand it to our wives—they'll get it anyway.

*

Many a husband who runs the show has a wife who writes the script.

*

Police seeking a foolproof lie detector should investigate the potential of the average wife.

*

UNDERSTANDING WIFE: One who has the pork chops ready when the old man comes home from a fishing trip.

*

GIRLS: If your husband starts dictating letters each time you sit on his lap, it's time to start asking questions.

*

Any man who thinks his wife doesn't understand him ought to be congratulated. He's married to a woman who knows how to keep a secret.

*

If a wife doesn't know whether her husband is man or mouse, she should keep her trap shut.

*

When a wife has laryngitis, it's like watching television with the sound turned off.

*

A man wouldn't mind his wife reading him like a book—if she didn't insist on doing it out loud.

*

When a wife is set in her ideas, her husband might as well sit on his.

*

Candy and flowers will do one of two things to a wife. It'll make her happy—or suspicious.

*

The point at which a wife will most likely meet her husband halfway is at a good restaurant.

*

It's been said that in some parts of Africa a man doesn't know his wife until he marries her. The big question here is: Why single out Africa?

*

A recent survey showed that single women enjoy fiction more than married women do; but that's understandable, because most wives hear too much of it.

*

Whenever a man gives his wife a lecture on extravagance, there are usually some changes made—he gives up smoking.

*

Mighty few things are nicer than a wife who likes to cook—and can.

*

For a person who never knows what she wants, the average wife is surprisingly adept at getting it.

*

Husbands have to be mighty shrewd when it comes to wives. For example, they'll never have any trouble hiding extra money if they hide it in the clothes that need fixing.

*

All a man has to do to take a chip off his wife's shoulder is to put a new hat on her head.

*

The way we figure, when a wife is watching, that's a bad time to have a good time.

*

There are some wives who are irritable at times and the least little thing will set them off; others are self-starters.

*

Nothing reminds a wife more that there's work to be done around the house than to see the old boy sleeping.

*

If a fellow really wants to learn do-it-yourself fast, all he has to do is criticize his wife's cooking.

*

WIFE: The reason a man can't afford to let the grass grow under his feet.

*

Why is it that a wife will always look at her husband when she says she loves the simple things in life?

*

Wives are available in every shape, size and temperament imaginable. Thank heaven most of us end up possessing just the right ingredients to make life worthwhile.

*

When a wife isn't boss of the house, it's probably because she has children.

*

Many a wife will back her husband—right into a corner.

*

When a wife starts talking to herself, it doesn't necessarily mean that she's losing her mind. It could simply mean that the old man is reading the newspaper.

*

Wives who wake up with a grouch every morning should try letting him get his own breakfast.

*

The average wife remembers when and where she got married. What escapes her is why.

*

The greatest mystery of all is how some wives can keep a clean house with all the dirt they pick up in the neighborhood.

*

If any of you fellows think the other guy's wife is so sweet and never gets ruffled or spiteful, just go along home with him sometime for dinner when she doesn't know you're invited.

*

FACT: When your wife treats you cold, it means she's plenty hot.

*

Some wives spend most of their day in the kitchen; not that they do much cooking, but that's where the phone is.

*

The only thing the average wife will admit she *doesn't* know is why in the devil she married her old man.

*

It must be wonderful to be a wife. Just imagine knowing that every time there's an argument, you're going to win.

*

Any time a wife decides to suffer in silence, you can be doggone sure the old man will hear about it later on.

*

Many a wife who is a live wire often shocks her husband with the clothes she's charged.

*

Wives with an inferiority complex can cure it by being sick in bed for a day and letting the old man manage the household and the youngsters.

*

Most wives don't ask for too much out of a life—just a roof over their heads and a chance to raise it once in a while.

*

I bet there isn't a wife living who doesn't secretly believe that her husband had terrible taste in women—until he met her.

*

When a wife serves her husband a nice, thick, juicy steak, it doesn't necessarily mean that she wrecked the car, went on a shopping spree or overdrew the checking account. She just may have run out of leftovers.

*

The hand that rocks the cradle rules the world; and the hand that darns the stockings is usually the one that socks the old man.

*

Whenever a man wants his wife to sit up and take notice, all he has to do is talk in his sleep.

*

It's always easier for a man to arrive at a firm conclusion about a problem after he knows for sure what his wife thinks.

*

Adam was the only man who could be sure about his wife—and even then a snake entered the picture.

*

Wives are sometimes as hard to manage as a greased pig.

*

You can't always tell what makes a man tick until you meet his wife. She may be the works.

*

There are some wives who are always willing to talk things over—and over and over and over.

*

Why is it that a wife will have nothing to say when you're in the room with her, but the minute you're at the other end of the house, she's full of questions?

*

A lot of husbands may know what makes their wives tick, but they can't figure out what winds them up.

*

They may sputter around like the spatter from a kettle of boiling grease, but there's nothing short of an X-ray machine that can see through a man like the average wife.

*

Some wives have an electric eye. Every time the old man walks in front of it, her mouth opens.

*

Whenever a modern wife refers to her husband as a jewel, you can be sure she's got him around her finger.

*

When you consider all the pants pockets and bankrolls, wives certainly go through a lot for their hubbies.

*

Truth may be stranger than fiction, but there are times when they sound pretty much alike to a wife.

*

A wise man may disagree with his wife, but only a fool lets her find it out.

*

Many a man has his nose to the grindstone because his wife has hers in the air.

*

A wife may not have much to say, but that doesn't keep her from talking.

*

A man doesn't have to be a football expert to know that a halfback is what he doesn't get when he turns his salary over to his wife.

*

Outside of the girls who fear spinsterhood, about the only females who spend most of their time looking for husbands are wives.

*

WIFE: A person who sits up with you when you're sick—and puts up with you when you're not.

*

A lot of husbands who continue to call their wives "the little woman" haven't looked lately.

*

A thoughtful wife these days is one who finds out what her husband would like for dinner, and then finds a restaurant that serves it.

*

Computers aren't so wonderful. They can give you the answers but not the problems. A wife can give you both.

*

It isn't so much what an angry wife says that hurts— it's the number of times she says it.

*

Some men quit listening to their wives long ago— but she's still talking.

*

ADVICE TO HUSBANDS: If your wife doesn't treat you as you deserve, be thankful.

*

Wives are unpredictable. You never can tell what they'll be spending too much for next.

*

When some wives kiss their husbands good-bye in the morning when the old boy is on his way to work, they may mutter, "Good-bye, dear," but what they really mean is, "Go fetch, boy, go fetch!"

*

Some wives are perfect lambs. Whenever the husband makes a suggestion, the answer is, "Baa!"

*

When a man comes home and asks his wife how she spent the day, it's like the little Dutch boy taking his finger out of the dike.

*

Waiting for some wives to finish talking is like looking for the end of a roller towel.

*

Since a woman's life is usually longer than a man's, wouldn't you think the average wife could wait about having the last word?

*

The faces of some wives light up when they see their husbands. The only trouble is that while their faces light up, their eyes snap fire and their cheeks burn with rage.

*

The only trouble about a wife briefing her husband is that it's seldom brief.

*

Really and truly wise is the wife who can make her husband believe that he is the head of the house, when in reality he is nothing more than the chairman of the entertainment committee.

*

The sudden entrance of a wife has caused many a secretary to change her position.

*

Who says that women can't take a joke? Just line up some of the husbands and give a good look.

*

Would you believe the average wife wastes four months of her life and 1,742 cubic feet of breath just asking her husband what he wants for dinner?

*

Some men allow their wives to spend money like water—drip, drip, drip.

*

Many a wife is a brilliant talker whom guests could listen to all night; her husband has to.

*

The most dangerous weapon in the world is an unhappy wife with a charge plate in her purse.

*

When a wife starts calling her husband "my precious lamb," you can take it for granted that she's about to pull the wool over his eyes.

*

A man's wife may not be the only woman he ever loved, but she's the only one who made him prove it.

*

One of the best ways for a wife to get her husband to tell her about his business is to begin talking about a new car for the family.

*

You can believe it or not, but the best check-writing machine was made from Adam's rib.

*

A wife shouldn't expect her husband to buy her all the finery that her father did. After all, her husband isn't trying to marry her off.

*

If you think those old time western gunfighters were quick on the draw, just open a joint savings account with your wife.

*

A man doesn't mind his wife coming from a fine old family—as long as she doesn't bring them with her.

*

When a wife suffers in silence, it's probably because she's alone in the house.

*

A musical sound to many a wife is the dishes being done by the old man.

*

Every wife has the problem of keeping her figure—and her husband's problem is to figure her keep.

*

A lot of wives were just as unreasonable before marriage as they are after, only then their husbands labeled it "being cute."

*

There is absolutely nothing that makes a wife feel more married than to notice, after she gets to church, that she smells more like waffles and bacon than her favorite perfume.

*

WIFE: A man's remote control.

*

Women

A wise woman sometimes takes leave of her husband just long enough to increase his appreciation—but never long enough for him to seek consolation.

*

The women the men toast are the ones the other women roast.

*

FACT: Women are always getting men into trouble! For example, look what an easy time Adam had until Eve ate him out of house and home.

*

Only a few women have the knack of really making something of a man, but all of them insist on tinkering.

*

Show me a man who says he understands women, and I'll show you a man who's in for a big surprise.

*

The way to a woman's heart is through the jeweler's window.

*

Woman was created from the rib of a man—so the good book says—and she's been ribbing him ever since.

*

According to evolutionists, it took nature millions of years to make a man out of a monkey—but a woman can reverse the process in a jiffy.

*

Permitting a woman to have the last word doesn't require courage, but it sure takes a lot of patience.

*

Women don't really change their minds very much. Ask one her age and she'll probably give you the same answer for years.

*

Any man who claims he can read a woman like a book is probably a mystery fan.

*

According to the poet, "Man wants but little here below"—and all a woman wants is something that tastes good, satisfies her appetite and isn't fattening.

*

There are two things all women fall for, regardless of age—a new hat and a whistle.

*

If you want to learn more about women, just get yourself a nifty convertible and you'll be surprised at what you'll pick up.

*

Some women, when they quarrel with their husbands, become hysterical; others become historical and rake up the past.

*

An intelligent woman is sure to be the center of attraction. But then so is anything else that is rare.

*

A woman's no is subject to modification,
And therein lies a young man's education.

*

No man can understand a woman—but some certainly have a lot of fun trying to.

*

It never hurts a man to call a woman beautiful—when she's in the kitchen.

*

Some women take a man for better or worse; others take him for all he has.

*

When a woman wears something light, she's sure to have a heavy date.

*

Sometimes a woman is afraid of a mouse—until she marries one.

*

The best way to get a woman's undivided attention is to tell her something that is none of her business.

*

It's no use trying to understand a woman. Even if you did, you wouldn't believe it.

*

Never underestimate the power of a woman—or the weight of her thumb.

*

Women can talk themselves out of just about anything —except a telephone booth.

*

When a woman fires a pound of sarcasm at a man, it weighs a ton when it hits him.

*

Some fellows may say that women are a dime a dozen, and they could be right. But it's when you cut the number down to one that it starts to cost you.

*

They sit up for their husbands so they can sit down on the bum when he comes home.

*

Experts tells us that after forty, a woman's views get broader—but that isn't all!

*

The trouble with women is, you please 'em and please 'em, but doggone it, they just won't stay pleased.

*

When a woman gets steamed up and boils over now and then, it's her husband who gets cooked in the process.

*

Nothing can vex like the opposite sex!

*

The average woman can put more in one look than a man can put in a whole book. And by keeping her mouth shut for fifteen minutes she can make a man spend the rest of the day wondering what she said.

*

This you'd better believe: A girl can dial a wrong telephone number and nurse it from a conversation to a date, to an engagement, to a marriage and a honeymoon, to a life of wedded bliss and all the time make the fellow believe that *he* was the aggressive one.

*

Since the dawn of history women have been a mystery.

*

At the Creation woman was only a side issue; now she's the whole works.

*

Whenever a woman gets a man in her grip, he's in the bag.

*

It takes a woman to take a man twice her size, wind him around her little finger, make him lie down, roll over and be a good dog.

*

Don't believe that every sad-looking woman has loved and lost. She may have gotten him.

*

TOAST: Here's to the women who made us men what we are today—and just look at us.

*

Say what you please, a woman is still a creature who dresses for men's eyes and women's eyebrows.

*

FACT: The first Adam-splitting gave us Eve, a force which men in all ages have never quite gotten under control.

*

Women and guns are alike—neither are to be fooled with.

*

It's been said that women are an improvement over men. Maybe so, and maybe that's the reason so many men stay out late at night—they're looking for improvements.

*

A woman is like a clock. Pretty hands, pretty face, pretty movement, and hard to regulate when they get out of order.

*

It's been said that a woman is nothing more than a rag, a bone and a hank of hair. Maybe so, but you'd be surprised at some of the crazy combinations they can make out of that!

*

Women are great mathematicians. They divide their age by two, double the price of their dresses, treble their husbands' salary and add five years to the age of their best friends.

*

There's one thing to be said about the opposite sex, and that is: Boy, can they ever be opposite!

*

Why is it that a woman will wait up for her husband until three o'clock in the morning just to ask him where he's been and what he's been doing when she's determined right from the start that she isn't going to believe a dog-gone word he says?

*

Women are unpredictable! You never know just how they are going to get their own way.

*

God made man and rested. God made the earth and rested. Then God made woman, and since then no one has rested.

*

Men: Just because a woman forgives you doesn't mean she isn't going to tell you about it for the rest of your life.

*

When God made woman He gave her every quality— a beautiful body, an engaging smile, a pretty face, a gorgeous head of hair, an attractive forehead, two sparkling eyes that twinkle like stars in the skies, a cute nose, a well-rounded mouth—then He stuck in a tongue and loused up the whole thing.

*

Fellows: You never understand a woman before you marry her, and afterward you only *think* you do.

*

Our private opinion is that women are a problem—but they're the kind of problem men like to wrestle with.

*

About the only way a man can have the last word with a woman is to chisel it on her tombstone, and that's exceedingly difficult, because it necessitates his outliving her—and a woman is one of the hardest things in the world to outlive.

*

There's nothing wrong with women drivers that can't be fixed by a good garage mechanic.

*

Male antipathy to women drivers is nothing new. In 205 B.C., the Romans passed a law banning women from driving chariots.

*

I suspect that the best way to get women to drive more carefully is to remind them that if they have an accident, the newspapers might print their real age.

*

Many a man has saved a lot of lives by *not* driving the way his wife told him to.

*

Teaching your wife to drive is the easiest way to lose control of your car.

*

A traffic engineer once said: "Stout, middle-aged women are safe drivers as a rule." It's surprising, even amazing, to learn this country has so many safe drivers.

*

Let's not be too hard on women drivers. After all, all they expect when they're at the wheel is for traffic to roll aside for them the way the Red Sea did for the Israelites.

*

Those of us who think women drivers aren't as good as men just don't realize how difficult it is to drive in the middle of the road.

*

Hell hath no fury like a woman driver in an auto accident.

*

Some of the girls drive as though their car came equipped with the right-of-way.

*

There's many a woman has put her husband back on his feet—when she wrecked the family car.

*

A woman driver can be very healthy, and still take a turn for the worse.

*

The worst women drivers you'll ever meet are in a crowded supermarket.

*

Statistics show that women drivers have fewer accidents than men, but that's easy to explain. Everything gets out of their way except telephone poles and garage doors.

*

Giving the girls the right-of-way isn't a matter of chivalry these days; it's just obeying the law of self-preservation.

*

A woman has two advantages over a man when it comes to driving a car. She not only can drive from the rear seat, but from either side of the front seat.

*

Would you believe that 51 percent of the nation's drivers are women? And that's only counting the front seats!

*

There's a lot of women drivers around the countryside with their husbands at the wheel.

*

MIDDLE-OF-THE-ROADER: A woman driver.

*

When a man is teaching his wife to drive, his instructions are: "Go when the light turns green, stop when it turns red—and take it easy when I turn white."

*

Guided missiles aren't new—not when you consider the woman driver.

*

It's hard to understand a woman motorist—you never know what she's driving at.

*

Reference to a woman driver could mean one who plays golf, handles a car or dominates a husband.

*

Some women are excellent drivers. Their only trouble is in starting, stopping, turning, parking, signaling and things like that.

*

Women drivers and pedestrians have one thing in common—they're both being run down.

*

Most any man would give a woman driver a good half of the road—if he could just be sure which half she wanted.

*

After she's parked her car, her big problem is which of the three parking meters she should put her dime in.

*

The thing that most women drivers dislike about parking is the noisy crash.

*

Most women get terribly upset over how close the fellow up ahead is driving to her.

*

The driving habits of some women are greatly improved. Now the husbands only have to have the car repaired, instead of replacing it.

*